This short but substantial book by Glynn Harrison sounds a profoundly prophetic voice to the church in the twenty-first century. He challenges us to stop behaving like terrified rabbits caught in headlights, or some form of collective Christian Rambo out to destroy all opposition. Instead, he calls us, like our Lord, to tell the 'better story' we have been given, with kingdom joy and excitement. Who knows? If the church takes up his challenge, we could change the world.
Lis Goddard, Vicar of St James the Less, Pimlico, London, and co-author of The Gender Agenda

A really first-rate piece of work on a most important topic. The style is warm, persuasive and engaging. The content is clear, incisive and wise. We really need this book! Glynn Harrison has served the church and wider society very, very significantly by writing it.
Julian Hardyman, Senior Pastor, Eden Baptist Church, Cambridge

This is a timely book that realistically and graciously raises important issues for the church today. Ending on a positive note by telling a better story, it should encourage church leaders as they seek to teach both truth and grace.
Nola Leach, Chief Executive, Christian Action Research & Education

In this nuanced and stimulating book, Glynn Harrison calls us, as a Christian community, to understand and contribute to culture and human flourishing in the light of our rapidly changing world. I commend *A Better Story* to all who want to respond seriously to the challenges and opportunities of our day.
Amy Orr-Ewing, Director of the Oxford Centre for Christian Apologetics

Glynn helpfully assists us in navigating a minefield of explosive and emotive issues with clarity and wisdom. He shows why and how the sexual revolution has transformed the thinking of so many, and yet how it has failed to deliver on its grand promises. In its place he tells a beautiful story of where our sexuality is designed to lead us and where all our longings can find ultimate fulfilment. I cannot recommend this book highly enough. Every Christian facing these issues should read it.
Michael Ots, evangelist and author

In a superficial culture where almost everything revolves around feelings and sensations, this book is like fresh water in the dry desert. If this refreshment has to do with a sensitive topic like human sexuality, then we have to welcome it as a most important contribution to contemporary reflection on the subject. Glynn Harrison combines deep and solid thinking with warm empathy as he explains 'a better understanding, a better critique, a better story' of a 'new' revolution. The abundant life that Jesus spoke about reaches all areas, including sex. For this reason, I am delighted that the author's ultimate goal in this work is 'to proclaim the Christian good news about sex'.
Pablo Martinez, psychiatrist, author and Bible teacher

Glynn Harrison's acute cultural analysis and inspiring presentation of the Bible's teaching provides a superb model of how orthodox Christians should address the subject of sex and marriage today. He demonstrates that the legacy of the sexual revolution is not the freedom and fulfilment it promised, but isolated individuals and broken communities. And he shows that the Bible, by contrast, points to a greater vision, a better story and a deeper love that, rightly understood, will capture hearts and inspire costly obedience, for the good of all and the glory of God.
Vaughan Roberts, Rector of St Ebbe's, Oxford, and Director of The Proclamation Trust

This is a wonderful book – clear and compassionate – a book I have wanted to read for a very long time, but no one has written it until now. Glynn maps out the extent of the sexual revolution, what's good about it as well as what isn't, and sets out how we can be confident in God's intention and gift in a way we can celebrate and commend to our unbelieving culture.

If I could afford to, I would send it to all bishops, presbyters and any other Christian leader. Please read it in your group or church; please be prepared to work through the ways it will help you flourish in God's good gift. Let this book take you to the breadth, length, height and depth of Christ's love, and help you to share that love with those who don't know it exists.
Keith Sinclair, Bishop of Birkenhead

A BETTER STORY

A BETTER STORY

GOD, SEX & HUMAN FLOURISHING

GLYNN HARRISON

INTER-VARSITY PRESS
36 Causton Street, London SW1P 4ST, England
Email: ivp@ivpbooks.com
Website: www.ivpbooks.com

First published 2017
Reprinted 2017

British Library Cataloguing-in-Publication Data
A catalogue record for this book is available from the British Library.

ISBN: 978–1–78359–446–7
eBook ISBN: 978–1–78359–451–1

Set in Dante 12/15 pt
Typeset in Great Britain by CRB Associates, Potterhanworth, Lincolnshire
Printed in Great Britain by Ashford Colour Press Ltd, Gosport, Hampshire

Inter-Varsity Press publishes Christian books that are true to the Bible and that communicate the gospel, develop discipleship and strengthen the church for its mission in the world.

IVP originated within the Inter-Varsity Fellowship, now the Universities and Colleges Christian Fellowship, a student movement connecting Christian Unions in universities and colleges throughout Great Britain, and a member movement of the International Fellowship of Evangelical Students. Website: www.uccf.org.uk. That historic association is maintained, and all senior IVP staff and committee members subscribe to the UCCF Basis of Faith.

CONTENTS

PREFACE

Some of my friends will say that I've been 'very bold' to write this book. What they mean is 'rather you than me!' In the current climate a misleading phrase here, a quote torn out of context there, and you will soon attract the attention of the Twitter mob.

But when a friend or colleague discovers that I'm a Christian, one of the first questions often asked is: 'So what do you think about gay marriage?' Or they express curiosity about some other issue connected with Christian attitudes to sexuality and marriage. And yet, compared with the range and quality of resources to help us respond to other apologetics issues such as science and faith, we remain relatively poorly served in this area.

And so I am throwing my hat in the ring. This book is my attempt to say why I think traditional Christian teaching on sex, marriage and human relationships is good news for today. It's simply an introduction, of course. There's much more to do. But I hope it will buttress the confidence of some, and spur on others to produce something better. We need a new generation of young, media-savvy Christian apologists, who will overcome their fears, get down to some intellectual spadework and proclaim the Christian good news about sex. Maybe my stumbling efforts will help stir more into action.

I want to say a big thank-you to all those who have inspired and encouraged me in this project, too many to mention by name. I'm especially grateful to the many individuals who have opened their hearts to me, over the years, with their own sexual struggles. It has been a privilege to walk alongside you. I'd also like to thank Julian Hardyman and Michael Ots for their feedback on the manuscript, and some academic colleagues for their invaluable comments. I'm grateful to Eleanor Trotter, my editor, for her patience, wise advice and unflagging support, and to Kath Stanton for her superb help with my mangled grammar. I'm indebted, too, to Amy Harrison who gave a hugely helpful critique and review.

Finally, I want to thank my long-suffering wife, who has been a stimulating and inspiring conversation partner throughout this process. I may write and speak about the importance of children and family, but she shows me what that means and what it really looks like. So this is for Louise, my friend, inspiration and one-flesh soulmate.

Glynn Harrison
Bristol, 2016

WHAT LIES AHEAD

Set in Ireland in the 1960s, the hit movie *The Magdalene Sisters* follows the fortunes of four young women incarcerated under a brutal regime of po-faced nuns running one of Ireland's infamous Magdalene laundry asylums. Named after Mary Magdalene – who some people believed to have been a repentant prostitute – these laundry asylums for 'fallen women' operated across Europe and North America for the best part of 200 years.

The legal basis for putting women away like this was often painfully obscure. But regardless of legal niceties, the shameful spectre of raising a bastard child was usually enough to keep these women out of sight, and out of mind, sometimes for years on end. Many children were quietly removed and put up for adoption.[1]

Surprisingly, the last laundry asylum in Ireland did not close until 1996. I say surprisingly because by the end of the twentieth century – in the Republic of Ireland as elsewhere – a cultural revolution of attitudes to sex and marriage was well under way. Things were changing so fast that, just a few years later, Ireland would become the first country in the world to legalize same-sex marriage by popular vote. Over one-third of the country's births would soon be taking place outside marriage.[2] That figure would rise to nearly two-thirds in some parts of neighbouring Northern Ireland.[3] The old conventions of holy matrimony were collapsing so fast that one opinion columnist (protesting against tax breaks for married couples) would ask, 'Why should I subsidise other people's weird lifestyle choices?'[4]

Another recent film, *The Imitation Game* starring Benedict Cumberbatch, tells how the brilliant British mathematician and code-breaker Alan Turing was convicted of 'gross indecency with a male' in 1952. Offered a choice between going to prison and taking sex-suppressing hormones, Turing took the drugs. He died tragically of cyanide poisoning two years later.

Half a century later a Christian street preacher reportedly told a passer-by, as part of an exchange, that he believed homosexuality went against the Word of God.[5] On this count he was bundled into the back of a police van by three uniformed officers and taken to a local police station. Police took fingerprints, a retinal scan and a DNA swab, and locked him up for several hours before charging him with a public order offence.

On Christmas Eve 2013 Turing was granted a royal pardon.

The events dramatized in the above-mentioned films, considered against their historical aftermath, portray something of the scale of the cultural upheaval we have come to call the sexual revolution. In the space of just a few decades the Christian moral vision, which had buttressed the ancient institutions of marriage and family for centuries, effectively collapsed. And most people today would think good riddance.

Living in the shadow of this great revolution, those Christians who still cling to the old Christian morality understandably feel overwhelmed. As if from nowhere, the home team suddenly feels like the away team. Worse, after witnessing the junking of their moral convictions, they find themselves cast as an immoral minority, a kind of enemy within. Most Christians no longer feel comfortable even admitting to their beliefs in the public square, let alone advocating them.

Against this backdrop, many Christian leaders, bishops and evangelists look like rabbits frozen in the headlights. Compared with efforts to defend their faith against the onslaught of the New Atheists, few have much to say about sex and marriage that is faintly inspiring or compelling. And when they do feel forced to publish some kind of official statement, it reads more like the terms and conditions of a software upgrade than a manifesto for human flourishing.

You have to sympathize with them. High-profile Christian leaders and evangelists don't want their entire ministry hijacked by a slip of the tongue that brings down the wrath of the Twitter mob shouting 'hate-filled!' But if this is how the shepherds behave, think about how the sheep must feel. They smell their leaders' fear. Confused and ashamed, some young evangelicals have already begun salami-slicing their convictions about the authority of the Bible. Others, like their leaders, are keeping their heads down, hoping and praying that the whole dreadful business will somehow go away. But it won't. It just keeps on coming.

As if from nowhere, Christians whose views once occupied the mainstream of public morality suddenly feel *weird*. It's worse than that: they feel *guilty*. Guilty for holding views held to be degrading to the human spirit. Guilty that they belong to a faith accused of heartlessly pushing the most vulnerable and marginalized out into the cold. Guilty for having apparently heaped abuse on those whose only crime was being different. What happened to bring about such a paradigm shift? That is the question we are going to address in this book.

What lies in store

Before we get started, I need to say something about how much we can realistically cover. First, this book isn't written to try to convince you about the authority of the Bible in determining the boundaries of Christian conduct and discipleship. I am going to assume that the majority of my readers hold relatively traditional (let's call them 'orthodox') views on sex and marriage, but need help in relating them to the modern challenges of the revolution. If that isn't you, I hope you will carry on reading anyway to see what this could look like.

What do I mean by 'orthodox' views? For our purposes, I use this term to summarize the following cluster of beliefs:

- God intended marriage as a lifelong commitment between one man and one woman.
- Marriage isn't simply a human arrangement, but something sacred in God's eyes.
- God himself joins a man and woman together as 'one flesh'.
- This understanding prohibits all forms of sexual activity outside the marriage bond.

If you (more or less) hold to this moral stance, then for the remainder of this book I'll call you an 'orthodox Christian'. I am going to attempt to convince you, in the face of the challenges posed by the sexual revolution, that the Bible's teaching is still good news. In fact, I want to aim higher. I want to persuade you that its teaching is life for the world and the only true foundation of human flourishing.

Even after narrowing its scope in this way, a book of this size can barely develop an adequate analysis of the questions, let alone supply all the answers. There isn't room, for example, to excavate all the arguments about the social benefits of marriage as opposed to cohabitation. And we won't be able to delve into the complex challenges of transgender and the other 'hot-button' issues served up on today's smorgasbord of sexual identities. A little information can be dangerous. So I will try to highlight the key issues and then point you to resources that deal with them more adequately.

You will have seen from the Contents that this is a book of three parts. Part 1 tries to get to the bottom of why Christians are stumbling so badly, by making three core arguments.

First, I will contend that we are failing because we are not thinking. We haven't grasped the ideological coherence of the revolution or mounted an effective intellectual engagement. When intellectuals talk about something oddly termed 'queer theory', for example, we look away with mild amusement. When activists make the social case for equality and civil liberty, we seem bent only on defending our own. Over and over we have failed to get to grips with the arguments that have made the vision of the revolution so plausible to so many ordinary people. We shall need to grapple with some difficult concepts in the early part of the book, but grapple we must. And I promise you, if you can stick with the earlier culture analysis, it gets easier as you go along!

Second, I will say that we have failed to grasp that the revolution has a positive *moral* vision of its own. Christians expected to be able to portray their opponents as moral anarchists bent on depravity. Instead, their opponents cast *them* as the degenerates. Far from portraying a Dantean nightmare of unfettered debauchery, the apologists of the revolution cast an inspirational vision of compassion and equality. How should Christians respond when people view them as being so bigoted and uncaring?

Third, we must grasp the central role that narrative played in helping to secure the revolution's cultural dominance. The two films mentioned earlier are a wake-up call to the power of movie narratives in winning hearts and minds. We need to learn how narrative structures and formulas can be used to make a point of view appear more compelling and plausible. And then we must ask whether we have a story of our own to tell? And if so, what is it?

In part 2 we move on to consider how thoughtful, biblically minded Christians should react to these challenges and mount a more effective critique. Too often our incursions into public debate have sounded over-defensive, judgmental and out of touch. We answer questions that nobody is asking. How can we begin a critical engagement with the fallout of the revolution in a way that wins hearts and minds, and not just arguments?

In part 3 I will urge that it is time for Christians to regain our confidence, time to offer a better story of our own, a story told with conviction and vision. Let's begin by being prepared to take some criticism on the chin. The revolution had some important lessons to teach us, and we should be prepared to say so. Our churches often cradled a sexual shame culture, and we should own up. We were so busy building our moral vision around what we were against – impurity, fornication, pornography and the rest – that we forgot to ask what we were actually for. We need to come clean about that. Then, and only then, will we be ready to rediscover a new narrative for a new generation.

A new ending

We can't undo the past. Nobody can go back and start a new beginning. But anyone can start right now and make a new ending. That is the task that lies ahead. We must rediscover what Jesus' promise of 'life . . . to the full' (John 10:10) looks like in relation to sex, singleness and marriage. And then we must begin to tell our own story, a story charged with hope, optimism and grace. A story told with inspiration and passion. A story told in words, yes, but also one put on display in our lives, real lives lived in real families and real communities.

Finally, let's acknowledge the scale of the challenge before us. In today's world the revival of a confident, biblically rooted vision of human flourishing in the sphere of sex and relationships looks like a pipe dream. Our culture seems so far adrift of its Christian foundations that it is almost impossible to imagine it. But imagine it we must. As I write in the shadow of Good Friday, I'm reminded that nothing looked more impossible than that Jesus would rise from the dead. Believers have been here before. Countless numbers paid the price for what they believed in, some with their lives. If we truly believe that what we have been given is life for the world, it is our turn now to stand up and be counted.

Part 1

A BETTER UNDERSTANDING

1 REVOLUTION IS MY NAME

How radical individualism went mainstream

So how did we get here? How come that over just a few decades Western society stopped heaping shame on single mums and started pondering whether marriage isn't, after all, just another 'weird lifestyle choice'? What powered the paradigm shift of values and lifestyle we now call the sexual revolution?

First, let me define how I use the term 'sexual revolution'. I'm referring to the overturning and liberalization of long-established social and moral attitudes to sex that began in Western culture in the 1960s, and continues to the present day.

At the heart of this revolution sits the relaxation of the idea that sex is given for enjoyment within the commitments (including towards children) of marriage. But there has been a broader unravelling as well: sex is portrayed much more explicitly in literature and films; cohabitation has become the norm; attitudes to same-sex sex have been liberalized; pornography is mainstream; sadomasochism causes amusement rather than concern; and the idea of gender fluidity is everywhere. Nevertheless, the core of the revolution is the severing of the link between sex and marriage that for centuries occupied the mainstream of Western culture.

What caused this great unravelling? We can take two broad approaches to understanding what happened. The first is to explore changes in economic and social circumstances that were in play over this period. For example, putting the economic case, the retreat from marriage can be linked with the introduction of generous welfare benefits in the wake of growing post-war prosperity.[1] This undermined the need for traditional male 'breadwinners' and created a raft of new opportunities for women. Progressive de-industrialization and the rise of service industries also multiplied employment possibilities for women. And campaigns for the equalization of income between the sexes put yet more strain on the traditional roles that had shored up the institution of marriage. Women just didn't need men any more. Or, at least, they no longer needed them in the same way.

Other social and cultural developments built upon these changes. Second-wave feminism raised women's expectations of equality and sexual satisfaction further. Divorce laws were liberalized and, as more children were being successfully cared for in non-traditional relationships, couples lost the motivation to stick together for the sake of the kids. The collective outcome of these changes (as welcome as many of them were) was a weakening of the link between sex and marriage, and the unravelling of the idea of marriage as an institution founded on a 'for-better-for-worse' commitment of permanence.

The final nail in the coffin of traditional marriage was almost certainly the introduction of safe, reliable contraception. At a stroke, sex was uncoupled from childbearing and all the responsibilities that go with it. People's bodies were their own, and they were free to do with them as they wished.

Ideas that change the world

Besides these social and economic changes, an alternative approach to understanding the sexual revolution is to explore the influence of new ideas that were catching on at the time, especially new forms of individualism. What exactly is individualism? It's about the weight we attach to individual thought and action relative to the importance of authorities and traditional institutions. In other words, individualism is about the value of thinking for yourself versus what you are being told by other people. It's also something to do with the uniqueness of the individual, their rights and their individual value.

So there's much to celebrate in individualism. Many of today's civic freedoms and privileges are rooted in new ideas about the authority and the power of the individual that arose during the European Enlightenment of the late seventeenth and eighteenth centuries. It's good to think for yourself. The Christian doctrine that men and women are created equally and uniquely in God's image underpins this and all responsible forms of individualism. God cares about the individual, especially those who suffer oppression and injustice, and he calls us to fight on their behalf.

So what was so different about the 1960s? Previously, individualism had been about striking the *right balance* between individual thought and reason on the one hand, and external authority and the wisdom of tradition on the other. Now it was about *freedom from* external authority and the wisdom of tradition – all of it. The balance tilted decisively in favour of the individual, and with wide-ranging consequences. Freedom was about being freed from the moral and ethical obligations imposed by others. It was about being freed from big business and religious institutions. Perhaps most radically of all, it was about being freed from nature itself. It didn't matter that we did not yet know how to make these claims happen; it was simply enough to assert them. And if reality wouldn't fall in line quickly enough, then we would redefine reality itself.

Welcome to the world of radical individualism. Before digging into this idea further, however, let's return to the cultural context of the 1960s to see how this new thinking took hold.

The times they were a-changin'

Bob Dylan's iconic anthem of the 1960s: 'The Times They Are A-Changin'' pretty much summed up the spirit of the age. The times were indeed changing, and fast. Dylan's celebration of change told parents that their children were now out of reach and 'beyond their command'. And if they couldn't lend them a hand, they needed to get out of their way because . . . the times they were 'a-changin''.

But what kind of change exactly? Actually, nobody knew. It was pretty much change for change's sake, as Dylan's critics point out.[2] At the time of writing, well into his seventies, Dylan still occasionally performs that song. But when an elderly grandfather sings, 'Your sons and your daughters are beyond your command', what does that mean for today? Back in the sixties it meant telling square people to accept the fact that their children were hippies. But today it could mean ex-hippie old men like Dylan accepting that their children have become bankers or city lawyers. Or arms dealers or terrorists. And why not? Shorn of a moral vision beyond change for change's sake, like *Joseph and His Amazing Technicolor Dreamcoat*, pretty much any dream will do.

The dream of the Big Me

It turned out that any dream would do, provided it was *my dream*. The authority of the individual and the primacy of thinking for yourself were taken to a whole new level. 'Freedom!' was the watchword. Freedom from authority. Freedom from 'nature'. Freedom to be me – whoever 'me' happens to be, or wants to be.

What happened to wake up this dormant giant of a philosophy and embed it so powerfully in the popular imagination? Several cultural factors were in play over this time. First, there was the growing popularity and cultural penetration of TV, films and popular music. Enthused by what I was seeing on TV in the early sixties, for example, I remember deciding that it was time for a James Dean-style quiff/pompadour makeover. Soon afterwards, inspired by 'Fonzie' from *Happy Days*, I moved on to the hideous duck's tail. And then, before the hairspray had a chance to dry, the whole thing had to be dismantled and swept forward into a Beatle-style haircut.

It was all about being different. We didn't want to distinguish ourselves from one another, of course. That was part of the irony, because we all ended up looking the same. But we wanted to be different from *them* – the representatives of conformity (teachers, vicars and the like) who told us what was allowed and what wasn't and what was normal and what wasn't. Well, to hell with all that because we were experiencing the first intoxicating flush of the freedom to be ourselves. Or at least that is what we thought.

But TV, pop stars and the movies didn't simply furnish young people with trendy new role models. They were the co-opted handmaidens of burgeoning post-war consumerism. This was an era of growing prosperity, and much of the new money was heading into the pockets of working-class kids like me. Our sheer weight of numbers provided a vast new marketplace for the Mad Men of advertising: motorcycles and cars, clothes and accessories, hairstyles and gadgets . . . it looked like everything was being designed especially for us.

Author Steve Gillon comments, 'Almost from the time they were conceived, Boomers were dissected, analysed, and pitched to by modern marketeers who reinforced [their] sense of generational distinctiveness.'[3]

These marketeers made us feel different, original and new. Most of all, they told us we were *special*. Little surprise then that in the slipstream of media-driven consumerism, the 1960s witnessed the birth of the self-esteem movement and the growth of pop psychology. As I showed in *The Big Ego Trip*, the spin doctors of pop psychology assured us that boosting self-esteem would revolutionize well-being, help kids do better at school, and buttress against addiction and substance misuse.[4] It didn't just make you feel good, they said, it *made you* good – a better person. And psychology proved it. Thus, media-driven consumerism and the penetration of self-esteem ideology became the twin foundations supporting the dream of the Big Me.

With various twists and turns, over the next five decades this shifting perspective towards the individual strengthened its grip. In 2006 the respected UK Henley Centre for Forecasting reported findings from a tracking poll that had been posing the same set of questions for over twenty years.[5] Each year the pollsters asked, 'Do you think the quality of life in the UK is best improved by (a) looking after the community's interests instead of our own or (b) looking after ourselves, which ultimately raises standards for all?' Before the year 2000, the majority had chosen (a), that is, most people thought that the best way to improve the quality of life for everybody was to put other people's interests ahead of their own. With the dawn of a new millennium, however, the gap had closed. Now, a majority of those interviewed chose option (b) instead. For the first time in the history of the poll the majority of people believed in looking after 'me' first. It was this cultural transition *from we to me,* driven by the ideologies of radical individualism, that fomented the shifts in thought and behaviour we now call the sexual revolution.

In sum

To summarize, we began by referencing the economic and social changes (for example, the introduction of welfare benefits and the relaxation of divorce laws) that underpinned the revolution, before exploring the new ideology of self that drove it forward. But there are two important caveats. First, it needn't be an 'either/or' battle between these two approaches. Both perspectives are needed. In fact, they interact: our beliefs and convictions, our dreams and our imaginings build up and tear down social networks and institutions on the one hand, just as these structures mould and shape our thinking and imagining on the other hand. Human minds, and the culture they inhabit, co-create each other in a continuous loop of dynamic interaction. Culture and the psyche 'make each other up'.

Second, we need to re-emphasize the many positive benefits of individualism. The fight against inequality was energized by the tilt towards the individual. It gave a generation of women being subjected to psychological or physical abuse the courage to get out from under the vice-like grip of their husband's control. It brought women's skills and gifts into the world of commerce and governance. Everywhere, the little people – sexually abused, discriminated against, downtrodden by establishment elites – found the courage to stand up and fight for their rights. Wherever we come across the defeat of injustice and unfairness, Christians should be among the first to celebrate, because this reflects the heart of God himself.

But this brief chapter hasn't been about those forms of individualism that seek to strike a balance between the rights and responsibilities of the individual on the one hand, and the role of external authorities and the wisdom of tradition on the other. It has been about radical individualism's bid for freedom from all authority and tradition. It has been about the sovereignty of the individual.

Nowhere is this more noticeable today than in the sphere of identity and gender ideology. So in the next chapter we dig further into the big ideas that powered the revolution. I will explore how, in its bid for sovereignty, the self claimed the ultimate freedom – the freedom to define itself.

Key ideas in this chapter

- The sexual revolution refers to the overturning and liberalization of long-established social and moral attitudes to sex and marriage. It began in the 1960s and continues to the present day.
- Big social and cultural changes brought about by post-war prosperity and radical new forms of individualism interacted ('culture and psyche make each other up') to give birth to this revolution and then drive it forward.
- The general concept of individualism (the value and responsibility of each individual person) is grounded in Christian tradition. Provided it remains anchored in broader values of community and mutuality, individualism benefits human well-being and flourishing.

- Today's radical individualism, however, heightens the sovereignty of the individual over all other sources of authority. This has shifted our culture in favour of individualistic approaches to a wide range of issues, with far-reaching changes to how we think about morality and human identity.

2 THE IDEOLOGY OF THE REVOLUTION

How radical individualism changed the way we think

'If you want to change the world,' Martin Luther once said, 'pick up your pen and write.' He did, and the world changed.

The bloody history of the twentieth century alone seems proof enough of the power of ideologies to change whole cultures and destroy the lives of millions. Ideas matter.

Or do they? For example, which was of greater importance in recruiting the German people's allegiance to their Führer? Was it the ideas and arguments contained between the covers of Hitler's *Mein Kampf*? Or was it rather the coercive power of the Nazi propaganda machine and the mass hysteria of the Nuremberg rallies? Many people today think it's the latter, so before going further, let's try to figure out where the truth lies.

Ideas versus power

Much recent pushback against the importance of reasoned argument is rooted in the work of the philosopher Friedrich

Nietzsche. Writing in the second half of the nineteenth century, Nietzsche argued that there are no 'big facts' that are capable of commanding universal assent, only human interpretations of them. The facts that do manage to make it into the mainstream of popular culture are simply those serving the power plays of the cultural and political elites that stand behind them. There are no all-embracing concepts that can offer real meaning to life, only clever ideas in the hands of people with the power to make them stick. So if you want your ideas to gain influence, he argued, you need to gain power.

Karl Marx was another important opinion former in this area. If you want to understand why some ideas thrive while others wither on the vine, he said, you must look at their social context. 'It is not the consciousness of men that determines their being but, on the contrary, their social being that determines their consciousness,' he insisted.[1] In other words, people *think* their ideas mould their social conditions, but the reverse is actually the case: social realities mould our thoughts.

More recently sociologist Peter Berger introduced the concept of 'plausibility structures' into arguments over the relationship between ideas and power.[2] Berger believed that the ideas that thrive in a particular culture are those offered *plausibility* by the social conditions of the time. So, for example, if the respected and popular wife of an ex-Beatle campaigns for the idea of vegetarianism, this is granted greater plausibility than, say, similar comments made by an unpopular government minister. Berger argued that all kinds of social conditions – the endorsement of opinion leaders, the example set by attractive role models, conversations conducted in a tone that implies 'everybody knows this' – give plausibility to ideas, allowing some to blossom and flourish, while others are left to wither and die.

These insights – Nietzsche's will to power, Marx's social being, Berger's plausibility structures – are important because they deepen our understanding of the multiple factors that are likely to be in play when people change their minds. But I am not ready to surrender the case for the power of ideas – far from it. Influential thinkers such as Nietzsche and Marx were, paradoxically, influential *thinkers*. They were subject to the same social and emotional influences they believed distorted everybody else's ideas, but that did not prevent them from attempting to propagate their own. Neither were they shy about using reason and logic in an attempt to communicate what they wanted to say.

We cannot escape from reason. That is why we talk today about the influence of 'thought leaders'. That is why the influential TED lecture format is billed as a platform for new ideas and innovative thinking. That is why, when business leaders such as the perfumer Jo Malone offer advice based on hard experience, their message is clear: don't go with your gut instincts, *think things through*.[3] Whatever the social conditions or power structures that push some ideas forward in favour of others, ideas – all ideas – must finally be explained and defended in the court of human reason.

And so we mustn't abandon reason simply because we have learned how easily she can be fooled. On the contrary, these insights should motivate us to defend her role more vigorously. Those who subscribe to a Christian worldview have even greater motivation to defend the place of reason. The biblical concept of human beings created in the image of God means that we expect a meaningful correspondence between the reality that God has put us in, and our abilities to make sense of it through the gift of reason.

And so, while we should acknowledge that there is interplay between ideas and the culture that they inhabit ('culture and the psyche make each other up'), we will not understand the power of the sexual revolution unless we get to grips with its underlying ideology. So let's dig further into the rise of radical individualism that we highlighted in the previous chapter with two specific questions: first, how did the revolution change our concepts of flourishing? And second, how did it change attitudes to identity and the reality of our own bodies?

Digging further into the rise of radical individualism

1 Radical individualism and human flourishing

In the last chapter we saw how post-war economic prosperity, fuelled by media-driven consumerism, released a vast new range of opportunities for educational advancement, geographic and social mobility, and personal independence. Young people started travelling to places their parents had never seen. They attended universities and obtained degrees their parents didn't understand. They began to use words and coin phrases their parents had never heard. All this heightened a sense of having been liberated, set free, from the strait-jacketing of the past. Freedom was the word.

And then along came pop psychology and the new therapy culture of the 1970s. At a stroke, self-expression was transformed from a mindless act of defiance into a moral quest. It was no longer change for change's sake, or freedom for freedom's sake; it was freedom *for the sake of authenticity and becoming your true self.*

This moral quest isn't simply being honest about your inner feelings and thoughts. It is saying that when you express these inner realities truly, authentically, you work with the grain of *who you really are.* Expressing your inner self in this way, being who you really are, is about being fully human. It is your moral duty.

As a result, 'just be yourself' has come to be viewed as something much more important than simply pleasing yourself. It's about becoming a proper person: an authentic, flourishing, fully human person. When these ideas mushroomed in the therapy culture of Tom Wolfe's 1970s' 'Me Decade',[4] they seemed incredibly refreshing and inventive. But were they really that new and exciting? With hindsight, it turns out they were just another iteration of an ancient philosophy called Gnosticism. As so often happens on life's journey, look a little closer and you discover we've all been here before.

But what is Gnosticism?

Modern Gnosticism: old wine in new wineskins
According to theologian N. T. Wright, ancient Gnosticism has surged to become a 'controlling myth' of our age.[5] Prevalent in the early era of Christianity, Gnosticism was one of its most troublesome heresies. There is a lively debate about whether there was ever one 'thing' called Gnosticism, but Wright suggests that there were four elements that were common to all its different forms.

First, Gnosticism advances the idea of a dualism in which the world of everyday reality – of space, time and matter – is viewed as being secondary to a higher spiritual plane. Second, it conveys the need to distrust, even to despise, the everyday world of 'things' because these have been created by a low-level, incompetent or perhaps even malevolent deity. Third, the solution is to make your escape from this material world on to a higher spiritual plane where there is no matter. And fourth, your escape hatch is labelled 'gnosis', that is, *knowledge* of the essential secrets that you will find in the higher spiritual world. Crucially, the most important secret of all is about how to be truly, authentically *yourself*.[6]

So in the Gnostic worldview, the material world is essentially evil, an ugly outcrop of the fall or the misshapen handiwork of its malevolent creator. As a result, all the so-called 'natural' distinctions in the world – for example, the difference between male and female, or the notion of there being a natural order to human sexual relations – are at best illusory and at worst corrupted deceptions. All this belongs to the 'outer' world of society and religion, indeed the outer world of your own body. It's all irrelevant and deceptive.

So wherein lies your salvation? You need to find the escape hatch called 'gnosis' or *wisdom*. Wisdom is about being liberated from the false impressions of the material world. It's about rebelling against the natural order, a great refusal of reality in which the 'good' of the self is defined by the strength of its own defiance.

Now you may think this is all very well, but where is the link with today's radical individualism? Ancient Gnosticism was framed by a supernatural worldview, whereas modern modes of thought are framed by secularism and materialism. So what do they have in common? They share the deep-rooted conviction that the source of the self is found by looking within. They share a revolt against the external, against the body, against nature itself. Christians would say they both tap into a fissure that runs through the human heart – a revolt against God and the reality that he has created.

Nowhere is the link between ancient and modern forms of Gnosticism more visible than in the sphere of sexuality. In its ancient form, Gnosticism viewed sexual liberation as the road to flourishing more generally. In fact, the debasing of sex and the cultic celebration of promiscuity were seen as the best means for ordinary folk to trample on nature and become more fully human in the process. Fast forward to this example of modern-day Gnosticism taken from lesbian feminist activist Donna Minkowitz's *Ferocious Romance*:

> Pleasure without restriction. Vulnerability without exploitation. To me, to most of us, gay love means all these things and more – an ecstatic knowledge, almost a gnosis that sex is possible outside the horrifying thickets in which the rest of the culture has hedged it. And that we ourselves can get it! Visions of a totally satisfying oral bliss, what Ginsberg called 'Caresses of the Atlantic and Caribbean love', the mind-stealing kisses of 'human seraphim,' a physical joy beyond the bounds of anything most people experience, almost beyond the bounds of desire itself, my God! no wonder people fear us! But they should not fear. They should open to the Ultimate, as we have done.[7]

Heady stuff. Did you notice the conflation of sex with the spiritual quest for transcendence? Similar to its ancient predecessor, modern Gnosticism's cult of liberation is defiant, ecstatic, redemptive. Examples of this way of thinking (albeit usually more nuanced and muted) are everywhere around us, and nowhere more so than in Hollywood.[8]

Before we get too carried away with ourselves, however, we should recognize that Gnosticism's reach into most people's world, yours and mine, is rather less colourful. True, at one end of the spectrum, in seedy newspaper revelations of tarts and vicars, politicians and prostitutes, you can witness cameos of defiant debauchery on display. But in reality it doesn't fit with most people's everyday experience. Think about the perfectly happy cohabiting couple with a beautiful little girl who run the charity you are proud to support. Pictures of bacchanalian nights of sex on the kitchen table somehow don't ring true. Then there's the very nice, but rather boring, gay couple living next door. Their lives seem to revolve around cups of tea and walking the dog, rather than raunchy nights of ecstatic hedonism.

But the impact of Gnosticism is no less important for that. At a subtle level it has insinuated itself deep into the modern psyche with far-reaching consequences. In a steady, relentless drip it has achieved the erosion and dismantling of marriage as an institution given by God ('Hey, why not just live together first? What's so special about marriage?'); the deconstruction of the family ('comes in all shapes and sizes'); and the cultural dominance of the idea that 'just being yourself' is the road to success ('I realized that I needed to find myself'). And those who oppose these ideas are seen as bigoted throwbacks to a bygone era.

2 Radical individualism's war against reality

Let's turn now to our second question: how has today's radical individualism changed concepts of identity and, specifically, attitudes towards our own bodies? There is a link to ancient Gnosticism's distrust of external authorities such as religion or tradition here. But now this has deepened to embrace a distrust of *all* that is external, including our own body. In many ways, this is a war against reality itself, but especially the reality of our own body. This carries big implications for how we think about identity and gender.

Let me give you some examples. According to the *New York Times Magazine*, 2015 was the 'Year We Obsessed Over Identity'.[9] In December 2015 of that year a transgender father of seven children reportedly left his wife and family in Toronto to start a new life as a six-year-old girl.[10] A few months earlier Rachel Dolezal, a thirty-seven-year-old white civil rights activist accused by her parents of falsely portraying herself as black, continued to insist that she still 'identified as black'.[11]

The relatively new concept of 'trans-speciesism' entered many people's vocabulary for the first time when a twenty-year-old Norwegian woman, alleging the sensory powers of a cat, reportedly claimed to have been born 'in the wrong species'.[12]

I am not citing these examples to mock the individuals concerned. Filtered through sensationalist reporting, we have no idea of the personal stories that may lie behind them. I quote them because they illustrate one of today's most influential ideologies: the repudiation of given identity in favour of self-identification.[13] In the past, identity was viewed as the product of various givens that are hard to control: nationality, sex, family, culture and social class. The task was to make the best of what we had been given. Now we are encouraged to 'discover' our identity within, or to create our own identity in any way we like.

We see this most commonly in the area of gender ideology (closely linked to something called 'queer theory'). We need carefully to distinguish *gender ideology* from *gender dysphoria*. Gender dysphoria describes the persisting emotional and personal discomfort of a small minority of individuals who experience their sense of gender as being different from their birth sex. This is a complex personal issue calling for empathy and understanding. Those who struggle in this area are often confused, frightened and humiliated, but there are no reliable scientific data available to help cast light on what is going on.

Although we cannot deal with this complex issue in detail here, I raise it because the experience of people with gender dysphoria is often used to justify a radical new ideology about what gender actually *is*. But we mustn't fall into the trap that says you cannot have compassion for the former without signing up to the latter. We can be fully sympathetic to the complicated (and mysterious) experience of those who struggle with gender dysphoria, without buying into the new gender ideology that has been built around it.

What does this new ideology actually look like? In the past, people's perception of their gender (what is meant by male and female) was determined by their sex (based on physical characteristics, hormones and chromosomes). Today, however, some people are trying to argue that sex should be interpreted by the individual's inner perception of their gender. Of course, this may be one way of trying to help people who feel confused about their gender, but it does so at the cost of confusing everybody else. Further, as the examples above demonstrate, in today's world the logic of self-identification is being applied well beyond gender. When there is a conflict between reality and our perception of it, the modern approach is to say that it is our picture of reality that needs fixing rather than anything in ourselves.

The abolition of the Tao

In the history of Western thought it has generally been assumed that reality has some kind of order and meaning to it – something we can attempt to 'make sense of' by using God-given human reason. In his book *The Abolition of Man*, C. S. Lewis spoke of this order and meaning as 'the *Tao*'.[14] He chose a word of Chinese origin (meaning 'the way') because he believed this notion of there being a natural order to creation could be found in every major culture around the world.

According to Lewis, because reality has a natural 'way' to it, some of our pictures of the world are actually right and others are actually wrong, depending upon *how well they conform to what is there*. Our instincts should be to bring our feelings into harmony with reality, and not demand that reality be made to harmonize with our feelings. He put it like this:

> Certain attitudes are really true, and others really false, to the kind of thing the universe is, and to the kind of things we are. Those who know the Tao can hold that to call children delightful or old men venerable is not simply to record psychological fact about our own . . . emotions at the moment, but to recognise a quality which demands a certain response from us whether we make it or not. I myself do not enjoy the society of small children [but] because I speak from within the Tao I recognise this as a defect in myself – just as a man may have to recognise that he is tone deaf or colour-blind.[15]

Now obviously, this is not an easy task, and in a fallen world our perception of the world around us is open to distortion and error. We have to work at it, pool resources and think things through in the light of Scripture. But even allowing for this, we should still be able to appreciate how Lewis's general sense of *submission* to the reality of God's world is something that is deeply repugnant to modern Gnosticism. Today it isn't the individual that needs fixing, it is reality. And so the right to identify yourself – 'I identify as' – is fast becoming a defining feature of contemporary life. This is a logical outworking, the latest turn of the screw, of the radical individualism that has been driving the sexual revolution for decades.

As we draw this chapter to a close, I find myself looking for some serious theological engagement with these weighty issues, especially gender ideology and questions of human identity. Sadly, much of the fresh thinking in this area has been carried out in liberal theological circles, and evangelicals have been caught napping by the scale and speed of culture change in this area. Once again we are failing because we are not thinking. Clearly some theological spadework lies ahead in grappling with the revolution's ideology and then finding how to put it into a language that people can actually understand.

We began this chapter with a robust defence of the power of ideas. But we also acknowledged that people change their minds for other reasons as well, to do with cultural and psychological pressures. So in the next chapter we are going to explore how radical individualism began to affect how we moderns make up our minds about right and wrong by exerting pressure through these non-rational avenues. To do that, we are going to journey further into the world of social psychology and moral psychology. But I promise you, it's much more interesting than it sounds.

Key ideas in this chapter

- Even though the human mind is easily tricked and susceptible to emotions, ideas still have great power.
- Radical individualism is a modern form of ancient Gnosticism. Gnosticism is about discovering, and then expressing, the 'inner you' hidden beneath layers of cultural and religious control.
- The new Gnosticism says people act properly – that is, authentically – when they freely express their inner true self. The rejection of external authority and the free expression of sexual interests become a kind of moral good and source of flourishing.
- This way of thinking laid the foundation for gender ideology, a radical re-imagination of the meaning of bodily sexual differentiation. Gender ideology makes gender something located in people's inner feelings

rather than something grounded in their (untrustworthy) external bodies. In this worldview, being fully human and truly flourishing means going with your inner feelings, rather than following these externally imposed norms.

3 THE MORAL VISION OF THE REVOLUTION

How radical individualism changes the way we think about right and wrong

In early September 2015, as a surge of migrants and refugees escaping the war-torn Middle East threatened to overwhelm European aid agencies, the body of three-year-old Aylan Kurdi, a Syrian boy, was found washed up on a beach. Next day a heart-rending photograph of Aylan's body lying face-down in the sand appeared on the front pages of newspapers across Europe. The political landscape around the plight of refugees changed at a stroke.[1] Arguably, that one photograph did more to change people's perceptions, and government policies, than anything achieved previously by a stack of UN reports and endless streams of newspaper articles.

Ideas have power. But as this incident reminds us, emotions also wield great power. So the question is: when human beings need to make up their minds about moral issues, which is more important – the way they *think* about the problem or the way they *feel* about it? The last chapter made the case in favour of the power of ideas. But there is a strong body of research to show that when we make judgments about right and wrong, and especially snap moral judgments, 'gut reactions' are extremely important too.

Feeling fast and thinking slow

Getting to grips with the part played by intuitions and emotion is key to understanding the moral ecology of the sexual revolution. This revolution did not persuade Westerners to abandon morality; it showed them how to think differently about right and wrong. Or rather, as I will attempt to convince you, it showed them how they could *feel differently* about it.

Gut reactions – instinctive, quick-fire responses to moral questions – are powerful life-shapers. Think about a widowed grandmother living alone and now in her mid-seventies. Harbouring a prejudice towards gay people with more than a whiff of homophobia about it, she has held trenchant views about sexuality all her life and sees no reason to change them now. There's a strong visceral quality to her views: she looks away from TV images of two women kissing and wrinkles up her nose at talk of 'gay sex'. She doesn't have to work out her responses to these moral questions – her guts tell her what she believes, and you can see it in her face. In fact, when you ask her why she holds these views, it becomes clear that she has never really thought about it at all. She just knows it's wrong 'and that's the end of the matter'.

Social psychologists such as Jonathan Haidt, author of the *The Righteous Mind*,[2] and Daniel Kahneman, the Nobel Prize-winning author of *Thinking, Fast and Slow*,[3] have gathered vast quantities of data illustrating how much of what passes as thoughtful evaluation actually operates at this subconscious gut level. Haidt conjures a picture of a small man riding an elephant – the rider represents our rational, logical self, and the elephant our intuitive, instinctive self. Taking the example of our grandmother, when she screws up her nose at a sex scene on her TV, the elephant leans. The rider on top barely reacts at all. He doesn't need to: the elephant has already leaned. The upshot of this, argues Haidt, is that if you want to change somebody's mind, *you need to appeal to his or her emotional elephant as well as to the intellectual rider on top*. We will come across this metaphor again later, but first, what is this quick-fire gut-response mechanism actually *for*?

Gut-level decisions help us to make quick judgments without getting bogged down

It isn't difficult to work out why the ability to make snap judgments is advantageous. When the wind causes the bushes close to a gazelle suddenly to move, a rapid-response fear reaction is advantageous even if ninety-nine times out of a hundred it turns out to be wrong. But how can this quick-fire mechanism benefit us in the more sophisticated evaluations and decision-making of modern life?

Think about booking a holiday online or buying a new appliance. It's now almost routine to search out endless online reviews and customer feedback. Yet as you have probably already learned the hard way, more and more information can be too much of a good thing. As the number of options grows, so does the paralysing indecision that goes with it. Will it be this hotel with the larger swimming pool or that one with the better view? Shall we travel from this airport with cheaper parking or from the more expensive option nearby?

Now imagine what your life would be like if *every* decision, *every* reaction, had to be sorted through with the same detailed analysis that you used to help pick the best hotel or new washing machine. Life would grind to a halt. This is precisely what happens in a rare form of brain injury in which the link is broken between decision-making and the capacity to feel emotion. In effect, every decision is a strictly logical process with no 'gut instincts' in play at all. So what happens? Far from improving decision-making, the elimination of emotion results in victims making silly choices or no decisions at all.[4] They simply get too bogged down in the detail to make up their minds effectively. So emotions are important to decision-making, and our gut reactions help us cut through the undergrowth and get on with life.

But rapid-fire gut reactions can get us into all kinds of trouble as well. First, they can prop up lazy thinking, especially when we are faced with tricky moral questions. When thinking begins to feel like too much hard work, you can just go with your instincts. Emotions such as fear and disgust are much easier and quicker to tap into than the laborious process of sifting through complicated and contradictory ethical theories. They help us out when we don't really understand the issues too, allowing us to substitute our answer to the easy question (how do I feel about it?) for the tougher, more complicated one (what do I actually think about it?). That is essentially what is happening with our grandmother's response to gay sex.

Besides propping up lazy thinking, going with your gut can be dangerously stupid too. As we saw in the previous chapter, business leaders such as the perfumer Jo Malone argue strongly that if we want to avoid disastrous business decisions, we need to guard against letting our hearts rule our heads. And so, drawing these different strands together, it's clear there are both costs and benefits to having a gut-responsive system involved in moral evaluation, and it's just plain sensible to try to strike a balance.

The six intuitive foundations of moral reasoning

Let's turn now to concentrate on what all this means for the way we think and feel about big moral questions. Jonathan Haidt has produced a convincing body of research to show that our intuitive reactions to moral questions tend to operate broadly along six basic psychological systems, or foundations.[5] Each system evaluates a moral question from a different point of view. In other words, each moral system has a different question to ask, a different focus of concern. You can picture Haidt's six systems as lying on a spectrum as shown in the diagram here:

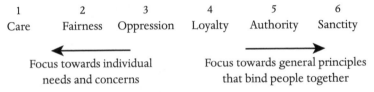

1	2	3	4	5	6
Care	Fairness	Oppression	Loyalty	Authority	Sanctity

Focus towards individual needs and concerns ← → Focus towards general principles that bind people together

Now let's see how each principle works by thinking about the moral question: 'Is it ever right to have sex in a threesome?' How would you make up your mind about that? Working through your six moral channels, the care/harm system on the left of the spectrum kicks in first, with the instinctive response: 'Well . . . is anybody getting hurt here? If not, we can probably feel relaxed about it.'

So far, so good. But notice how, as you work your way along the six-point spectrum, each of the remaining five systems looks at the problem from a different angle. So the next question is a concern for fairness ('is this unfairly benefiting one person more than another?'), followed by a desire to protect the weak ('is anybody being oppressed here?'). You will have noticed that these first three systems, on the left of the spectrum, have a focus on the individual – their safety, and their right to being treated fairly and equally.

The three systems on the right of the spectrum deal with more general moral concerns, focused on big principles that help to bind people together and keep everybody safe. Number six, at the far right of the spectrum, is concerned with the big sacred principles (such as the sanctity of life) which help protect the whole community ('are we meddling with a sacred principle here that could put the whole community at risk?'). Number five is concerned with respect for received wisdom and tradition ('what have our kind of people always believed about this?'); and number four with loyalty to those close to us ('would my view on this make me disloyal to people whose views I respect, and weaken community cohesion? Would taking part in a threesome involve disloyalty to anybody?').

There are two important points to note about Haidt's moral systems. First, these are mainly intuitive responses: we *feel* these questions in quick-fire gut reactions that happen faster than you can think.[6] Second, Haidt has shown that when asked to make moral judgments, people differ, often in predictable ways, in the relative weight they give to these six different gut-level responses. Those on the political liberal left, for example, consistently score most highly on those moral concerns connected with individual care/harm and equality/fairness – that is, those towards the left of the spectrum. So, thinking about attitudes to gay marriage, for example, those on the liberal left prefer to approach it with questions and concerns such as: 'if marriage is so good for heterosexuals, let's allow gay people to share in the benefits as well'; 'everybody deserves to be treated fairly: I'm for marriage equality'; 'gay people have been oppressed for too long – it's time to level the playing field.'

People who are more socially conservative, on the other hand, and those from non-Western cultures, score highly in respect for those responses towards the *right end of the spectrum*

– valuing loyalty, tradition and the kind of sacred values that hold people together and help protect everybody, rather than focusing on the few. And so, in relation to gay marriage, they use evaluations like: 'we are talking about the redefinition of marriage here – marriage is an institution found in every culture through all history, and we meddle with it at our peril'; 'it's no use trying to meet the needs of a subsection of the bees if you end up destroying the whole hive'; 'every kid deserves both a mum and a dad – we are experimenting with a whole generation of kids here.'

And so, depending on background, personality and religious convictions, some of us veer instinctively towards the right of the spectrum, and others towards the intuitions at the left of it. Or, to put it another way, some people's intuitive elephants lean to the left, while other people's lean instinctively to the right.

Which way does your elephant lean?

I want you to take part in a brief thought experiment with me now, although if you are about to have supper, you might prefer to finish this section later. A teenager from a wealthy and privileged background passes the entrance examinations for Oxford University. Soon after arriving, he decides that he will join one of the men-only dining clubs, notorious for their drinking and promiscuity. He is aware of rumours that the club he wants to join plays host to some rather extreme, indeed debauched, initiation ceremonies, but he doubts they are actually true. To his surprise, then, as part of the initiation ceremony, he is instructed to have sex with a pig's head.

Pause for a moment and examine your inner reactions to this story. When a similar alleged incident was included in an unauthorized biography of the UK Prime Minster, and splashed across the pages of most national newspapers, several million British citizens had to do precisely that.[7] Now, assuming that the individual in our fictional story decides to go ahead with the initiation, I want you to ask yourself whether you think there was anything actually morally wrong with his behaviour.

I am fairly sure that on first hearing the story, the vast majority of readers will have experienced an initial sense of revulsion – an instinctive, visceral feeling of distaste, disgust even. In all likelihood this emotional response will have preceded any rational thought or reasoned assessment of the circumstances portrayed in this story. This is the instinctive lean of the elephant – the split-second reaction of disgust that leaves us with no time to think. For most people, the strength of this reaction alone is enough for them to have made up their minds and caused them to screw up their nose and condemn the individual as a debauchee with too much time, and certainly too much money, on his hands.

But now I want to press my question once again. I want you to steady your elephant and allow me to talk directly to the rational rider sitting on top. On strictly objective, rational grounds, do you think there is *actually* anything morally wrong with this man's behaviour at the initiation party, and if so, what is it precisely? Think about it carefully and try to ignore your emotional response.

At this point opinions will begin to diverge. If you have been raised in Western Europe or the United States, and especially if you take a generally 'liberal' or 'libertarian' approach to life ('what people choose to do is up to them provided nobody else is getting hurt'), you are likely to take a relaxed, non-condemning line: 'Well, it's pretty gross and not the sort of thing I'd want to do myself, but hey, if he's not hurting anybody, if there are no innocent parties involved, then what people do in private is up to them . . . I'm with [tongue-in-cheek] Pope Francis on this one: "Who am I to judge?"'

Many people in Western culture would probably reach this conclusion. Although they share the initial sense of revulsion and disgust, when urged to think more carefully, they tend to judge in terms of the three foundations on the left of our spectrum: is anybody getting hurt, oppressed or being treated unfairly? And if not, well, 'who am I to judge?' Indeed, the stronger the culture of individualism and personal freedom, the weaker over time the instinctive disgust and revulsion becomes: 'Each one to his own! If nobody is getting hurt, what business is it of mine?'

If you happen to be reading this from a non-Western culture, however, or more likely if you have strong religious views about human beings made in the image of God, you have probably concluded that, regardless of your initial feelings, there is still something intrinsically wrong about having sex with a pig's head. It degrades the dignity of the person's divinely ordained humanity and violates both the natural ordering of human sexual interests and the right treatment of God's creation. For you that's the end of the matter. It's morally wrong, and this man should be ashamed of himself.

This simple thought experiment illustrates how people's approach to moral reasoning differs between, and even within, cultures. Westerners with liberal social attitudes tend to give prominence to the individualistic perspectives that care about harm, favour the individual's freedom to choose, and insist on fairness. People from non-Western cultures, and Westerners with socially conservative convictions, tend to favour the idea of objective principles of morality that say some actions are wrong because they are wrong, even if they don't appear to be hurting anybody. In contrast to social liberals, they favour sacred values such as the sanctity of life or the sacredness of the marriage bond because they believe these principles have universal application, whatever the personal circumstances of the individual. They hold to values such as personal loyalty, family commitment and love of tradition because they sense these provide the glue for binding communities together and preserving the 'common good'. They argue that it is no use trying to meet the needs of individual bees, or cater solely for 'bee minorities', if in doing so we destroy the whole hive.

Having surveyed the broad landscape of moral intuitions, we return now to ask how this helps us better understand the sexual revolution and what has been happening as Christians have struggled to respond to it.

The lessons from moral foundations theory

1 Over-reliance on moral intuitions supports lazy thinking and fosters bigotry

As we saw above, gut reactions can be the lazy person's escape route from difficult decisions: they allow you to substitute the answer to an easy question (how do I feel about it?) for the tougher, more complicated one (what do I actually think about it?). While this can be beneficial for the small stuff, for the big ethical and moral questions posed by the sexual revolution it can simply underpin bigotry. Recall the example of the grandmother we considered earlier: she simply picked up her attitudes as a child, much as you might catch a cold from the people around you, and these instinctive responses have shaped her life ever since.

2 Over-reliance on moral intuitions makes people vulnerable to social pressure and conditioning

Staying with our grandmother example, the problem with her emotionally based attitudes is that they are highly vulnerable to social and emotional pressures. As a result, people like her can sometimes 'switch sides' on the basis of socially mediated emotional conditioning, rather than thinking things through. All they need to do is substitute one set of reactions for another. Let me illustrate by developing Grandmother's story a little further.

On the face of it, Grandmother's views seemed pretty much set in concrete – until one fateful day. Out of the blue, a favourite teenage grandson comes out to her as gay. At first it's a no-go area in conversation, and the subject gets changed. Over the next few weeks and months, however, to everybody's surprise, not least her own, her views begin to change. 'He's a lovely boy,' she tells friends, 'he's taken a lot of bullying at school and he's going to get all the love and support I can give him.' Even more surprisingly, she begins to advocate for the rights and freedoms of LGBT people as well: 'If that is who people are, then what right do I have to tell them how to live their lives? Doesn't everybody just deserve to be happy?'

What on earth has happened to Grandmother's deeply held convictions? They have changed, quite radically, but she hasn't needed to do too much thinking about it. She has simply slid along the spectrum from right to left, substituting her previous feelings of disgust with new feelings of compassion. The whole process has been a relatively 'thought-free' zone: all she knows is that she loves her grandson, and her culture has provided her with some easy slogans ('doesn't everybody have the right to be who they are?') to oil the process of transition.

3 The rise of radical individualism has shifted people's moral intuitions towards the left of the spectrum

The rise of radical individualism has shifted the balance of Haidt's six moral intuitions decisively to the left – certainly in relation to sexual morality. Today's individualistic culture constantly nudges us towards the left because *these are the moral systems focused around individual needs*.

Individualism also allows us to feel more caring. It is much easier to experience compassion for the suffering of the flesh-and-blood individual sitting in front of you, than to express support for vague moral sentiments about the 'common good' or the 'sanctity of life' that seem to be hanging somewhere in the clouds. Let me show you how this works.

Here is an example of individualist moral reasoning during a debate that took place in the UK Parliament.[8] British legislators were considering whether to legalize a controversial medical intervention involving the transfer of mitochondrial DNA, in order to help a tiny number of children affected by a rare but devastating genetic disorder. The debate pivoted around the extent to which this treatment represented a form of genetic modification that tips us into the ethical minefield of 'designer babies' and 'three-parent embryos'. One Member of Parliament, a supporter of legalization, turned to those who had raised these principled ethical objections and said this:

> We are in a society where people are entitled to have their beliefs, and I respect those beliefs; everyone should be entitled to express their opinion. But this is about focusing on the needs of that small part of the population that I mentioned. I urge the House, in coming to a conclusion this afternoon, to think about those families, to focus on their needs and to

set aside general beliefs in the overwhelming interest of that
small part of the population who have suffered immensely . . .

The MP urges his opponents to set aside their 'general'
principles, such as religious convictions about the dignity of
the human person and the ethical limits on interfering in the
human germline, as well as their 'general' concerns about
potential damage to other innocent babies in the future. These
needed to be set aside in favour of the needs of individual
families being affected today. He invited his opponents to
'think about *them*', to *picture their suffering* in their minds. The
whole tone of the intervention portrayed his opponents'
'general principles' as being at best technically preoccupied,
and at worst heartless and uncaring.

This cultural shift away from 'general principles' to individualistic moral reasoning has been one of the greatest
achievements of radical individualism over the past half-
century, and nowhere more so than in the field of sexual ethics:
treat the individual well, and the rest will look after itself.

*4 We see all six moral systems perfectly integrated in the life
and character of Jesus Christ, and we are called to be like him
in our moral judgments*
These insights from moral psychology hold three important
lessons for Christians grappling with these cultural shifts.

First, our approach to sex and relationships must not be
allowed to rest solely upon gut instincts. Jesus roundly
denounced Pharisees whose orthodoxy was driven by disgust
and judgmentalism, and he would do the same today.
Christians need to get their thinking caps on. If their convictions can be shaken so easily by a good and kind friend who
is cohabiting perfectly happily with her partner and three
children, or by a young relative who bravely comes out as gay,

they were probably not worth having in the first place. Maybe it was just bigotry that fuelled them all along. Our evaluations need to be grounded in a much more serious engagement with the moral vision of the Bible.

Second, Christians often cave in to the sexual revolution because they haven't understood its moral nature and particularly its reliance on individualistic moral reasoning. They try to rebut its compassion and fairness (moral foundations one to three) with arguments from authority and tradition (foundations four to six). But in today's culture, people who possess no language of fairness, or compassion, or equality lose every time. So Christians need to find a language that connects their general convictions to their culture's individualistic concerns. In all this, once again, we are failing because we are not thinking. Or rather, we are failing because we are not thinking about *how we think about* these moral questions.

Finally, it isn't simply the research evidence furnished by moral psychologists that makes me believe that they are on to something: I am drawn to their work because, taken in the round, these moral foundations are reflected in the character and person of God revealed in Jesus Christ. Over and over again, in his personal encounters, Jesus integrated justice and compassion for the individual with uncompromising obedience to God's Word and his moral law.

Take the case of the woman caught in adultery. The Pharisees threw this woman at Jesus' feet and demanded that he address the situation in terms of the moral foundations lying to the right of the spectrum ('should she be stoned according to the Law of Moses, or not?'). Jesus' first response, however, comes in terms of the foundations on the left of the spectrum: 'Let any one of you who is without sin be the first to throw a stone at her . . . neither do I condemn you'

(John 8:7, 11). Then, as he sends her away, he reframes his entire response in terms of the foundations on the right of the spectrum: 'Go now and leave your life of sin.'

Here is the Christ-centred challenge for Christians today trying to get to grips with the sexual revolution. We must understand, and then incarnate, how the gospel deals with our broken lives with both conviction *and* compassion. The whole gospel puts on display the whole moral character of God. And we need to operate across all six channels not only because it's good science, but because it's good theology too. That is the challenge that lies ahead of us.

Key ideas in this chapter

- Emotionally charged, instinctive, gut-level reactions play an important role in the way we make up our minds about moral issues.
- While these gut responses help us to make everyday decisions without getting bogged down in too much analysis, they also support lazy thinking. And they can be dangerously wrong.
- People on all sides of the debates about sex often hold strong views based on gut reactions that are badly thought through. Christians (and their critics too) need to be more self-aware and prepared to think through their moral convictions.
- On matters of ethics and morality, radical individualism shifts people's gut intuitions away from those that uphold general sacred principles (such as the sanctity of life) towards those that respond to individual needs (such as compassion and concern for fairness). As a result, people's moral concerns often revolve around the needs of the few rather than those of the many.

- Orthodox Christians need to talk about general moral principles in ways that connect with people's individualistic concerns for compassion and fairness. In other words, they need to show how their moral convictions bring compassion, justice and fairness for the many, as well as for the few.

4 THE STORYTELLERS OF THE REVOLUTION

How activists used great stories to move people's moral elephants

> There was a boy called Eustace Clarence Scrubb,
> and he almost deserved it.
> C. S. Lewis, *The Voyage of the Dawn Treader*

What a great introduction to Lewis's book, *The Voyage of the Dawn Treader*. Just a few words and already we are gasping for more. Everybody loves a good story. Stories electrify the brain, fire the imagination and hook our deepest longings and desires. Jesus knew this. He took the simplest events – a shepherd leaves behind his entire flock to go looking for one lost sheep; a lone traveller gets ambushed and beaten up by thieves; a king throws a party that nobody wants to attend – and crafted them into compelling storylines with hard-hitting twists in the tale. Full of life-changing insights about the shadowy deceitfulness of the human heart, his stories pressed home how much is at stake in the choices we make about our lives.

So far we have seen how, with its unique brand of individualism, the revolution not only succeeded in changing people's minds about right and wrong, but it introduced big new ideas about identity, and made us think hard about the nature of reality itself. It took complicated and hugely controversial ideas and catapulted them into the mainstream of public life. So what was the secret of its success? The sexual revolution had a narrative. It didn't clutter people's minds with difficult facts or bore them with complicated academic details – it told them some stories instead.

The structure of a good story holds information in ways that seem to fit naturally with how the human mind works. Stories are sense-making devices that imbue our lives with meaning. They operate as powerful vehicles for the infectious spread of new ideas. The architects of the sexual revolution won over the popular imagination because they knew this. And so they started telling great stories like those in the films I used to introduce this book.

The entertainment industry is probably the revolution's most effective tool of cultural subversion. Talented and imaginative academic scholars, helped by some of Hollywood's best scriptwriters, took complicated ideas and melded them into the simpler structure of a narrative. This wasn't a cynical propaganda exercise – they believed in what they were doing. And so with riveting narratives about hypocritical politicians and fossilized bishops, pitted against outsiders and the oppressed, brave men and women finding the courage to be 'who they really are', they appealed to the moral instincts of ordinary, decent people. Instinctively, they knew about the power of stories to move the heart. Today we are beginning to understand how stories like this affect the human brain. Think about the following cameo:

Your brain and stories

'Ben's dying,' says Ben's father as he turns to camera with his two-year-old son playing happily in the background. Ben doesn't know that he has an aggressive brain cancer that will take his life in just a few months.

Continuing to talk to camera, Ben's dad tells us how hard it is to connect with his son when the end of his life is so near. When Ben's around, he says, it's especially tough trying to keep happy and stay joyful. But in the end he is determined to find the strength to be genuinely happy for his son's sake and to work to make him happy 'until his last breath'.

This moving vignette was used as part of a series of experiments carried out by the neuroeconomist, Paul J. Zak.[1] Zak researches the brain mechanism that helps explain how stories like this connect so well with our emotions, leaving us feeling more compassionate and generous. Zak discovered that after watching stories like this, people are more likely to be generous afterwards. Crucially, he found that a rise in empathy (the ability to understand a situation from within another person's perspective and to feel what they are feeling) was associated with an increase in a brain hormone called oxytocin.

There has been a lot of hype around oxytocin in recent years. It's a hormone made in the brain and variously dubbed the 'cuddle chemical', the 'moral molecule' and the 'bliss hormone'. Like all associations between a brain substance and a particular behaviour, people have leapt to unwarranted conclusions about cause and effects. Recent work has also questioned how accurate some of the measures used in these experiments have been.[2] So we should avoid getting too carried away.

Nevertheless, the balance of the evidence suggests that when researchers like Paul J. Zak talk about the brainpower of stories, they are on to something. Zak's work shows how a good story seems to 'hack' into the oxytocin system, with the result that we experience more empathy, compassion and, crucially, a greater sense of generosity.

What makes a good story?

But what is the secret of a 'good' story? In other words, what kinds of stories seem to be especially effective at hacking into oxytocin regulation? On the basis of blood samples taken before and after telling stories to subjects, Zak's work suggests the stories that most consistently boost oxytocin tend to be those that are strongly character driven. Crucially, those with a 'heroic dramatic arc' seem to work best of all.

Over sixty years ago the author Joseph Campbell inspired a generation of filmmakers and storytellers with his monumental book *The Hero with a Thousand Faces*.[3] Legend has it that George Lucas used Campbell's book as a foundation for his *Star Wars* adventures.[4] Campbell claimed that running through all the great myths of human cultures, there's a universal motif of struggle, adventure and heroic transformation. Great stories with the power to grab our attention employ a dramatic arc structure that goes something like this: a character struggles against overwhelming odds and seems on the edge of defeat; suddenly she discovers hitherto unknown powers or abilities; these new powers (or insights) enable her to triumph dramatically, and decisively; everybody lives happily ever after. Sounds familiar?

Let's return to the experiment involving Ben, the boy with the brain tumour.[5] Paul J. Zak developed an alternative video of the same father and son spending a day at the zoo, but this time there was no mention of cancer or death. Ben is still completely bald as a result of chemotherapy, but this time around his father simply refers to him as a 'miracle boy'. Ben's dad takes him to look at the animals in the zoo, but we don't know why we are watching or what we are supposed to learn from it. The point is that this second film, which lasts the same length of time, has no narrative structure – it is a 'flat' portrayal of facts rather than one with a rising sense of dramatic tension calling for resolution.

Zak and colleagues observed that subjects who watched this second film found it much harder to sustain attention. Measures of emotional involvement barely flickered, and much less oxytocin was produced. Afterwards, when they were invited to donate to a cancer charity, these subjects were less generous too.

How stories grab the attention and change people's minds

So what are we learning?

First, stories have the power to arrest our attention and grip the imagination. In a social media world in which everybody is staring at their mobiles, attention is in short supply, so an ability to break through the information noise grows ever more important.

Second, by increasing empathy, good stories open us up to the possibility of change. We have seen how stories capture our imagination by boosting the empathy-building hormone oxytocin. And when they are presented to us visually, their dramatic tension can be enhanced with music and sound effects. This, coupled with the fully immersive experience of a darkened theatre, means that the cinema-going 'surround sound' experience exerts even larger effects on the brain.

The neuroscientist Jeffrey Zacks (not to be confused with Paul J. Zak) has drawn together a body of research that illustrates the power of cinema going. In his book *Flicker: Your Brain on Movies*[6] Zacks shows how immersion in the visual/sound/sensory drama of the movies hacks into our *imitative instincts* as well as our emotions. So as you watch James Bond clinging to a ledge, 500 metres above a busy street below, your heart rate increases, your pupils dilate, and your muscles tense in sympathy. Your body as well as your brain becomes immersed in the story. Filmmakers have learned to turn up the bassline and use close-ups of the actors' expressions to create 'super-stimuli' that tug at the heartstrings. And because we are drawn sympathetically to heroes struggling against overwhelming odds, stories with a redemptive dramatic arc are especially effective at provoking the brain into readiness for change.

The philosophy of storytelling

The philosopher Charles Taylor has also argued (from a different perspective) that we do not store ideas about ourselves, and the world we live in, as a list of facts that accumulate in the memory ready to be rehearsed: we hold them at an imaginative, pre-conscious level, in the form of stories, myths and legends. Author James K. A. Smith, in a highly readable introduction to Taylor's work, has illustrated how this works in relation to today's dominant narrative of progressive secularism (the idea that everything is progressing forward because of secular values and ideas).[7] He suggests that people don't hold the ideas of progressive secularism as a list of facts, but rather as a story running in the background of their minds:

> There is a dramatic tension here, a sense of plot, and cast of characters with heroes (e.g., Galileo) and villains (e.g., [the 'medieval Catholic Church']). So if you're going to counter [these] stories, it's not enough to offer rival evidence and data; you need to tell a different story.[8]

In other words, you can't out-fact a story. You need to tell a different story. Or, we might add, a *better story*. And in today's world nobody tells a better story than the philosopher script-writers of Hollywood.

The power of real-life stories

Besides the entertainment industry, however, there is another avenue by which the stories of the revolution embedded themselves in popular culture: in the *real-life, heroic narratives of ordinary people* battling for their freedom. When the full horror of AIDS broke in the 1980s, there began to emerge incredibly moving stories of compassion and selfless care. Even as society recoiled, and some heralded a coming 'gay plague', ordinary men (they were mostly men) nursed their partners in circumstances that some of those calling down judgment upon them would simply have refused to con-template: they bathed their wounds, emptied their bedpans and fed their wasting bodies until finally they laid them to rest. Or rather, until they were forced to watch from a distance as their families laid them to rest.

This form of cultural embodiment can exert a powerful effect on hearts and minds. Tim Montgomerie, a columnist with the *The Times*, has written movingly of how, as a Christian, he came to change his own position on gay marriage. While offering prayer ministry during a church service one evening, he encountered a depth of love and grief in a man who had lost his gay partner, for which his orthodox beliefs had no convincing response:

> He had stood at the back of his soul mate's funeral as a distant mourner. He told me that he'd never felt lonelier. My eyes were now full of tears too. I cannot believe that Jesus Christ wouldn't have embraced and consoled that man . . .[9]

This is a deeply moving encounter. Of course, we can admire Tim Montgomerie's compassion and care for that individual, but still part company with a process of reasoning that manages to connect this experience to the case for redefining marriage. This is in fact a good example of how emotions affect the way we make up our minds about moral issues in a highly individualistic culture. But Christians must be prepared to acknowledge the many compelling examples of self-giving humanity, like this one, as the sexual revolution unfolded. They must be prepared not only to engage with the ideas that underpinned it, but prove that in the long run they are in possession of something even better. And that 'something better' must equally be seen in authentic, sacrificial lives of beauty and persuasive power.

Many of the key players in the sexual revolution understood the need for this kind of cultural embodiment. They showed that they were willing to swim against the flow. They braved the stigma of difference, marched the streets, formed pressure groups and conjured up the determination to show the world what love could look like. And if there's to be a Christian sexual revolution capable of turning the tide, it will need to do the same.

So far we have thought about the broad storytelling structure that carried the revolution's message and vision. Now let's listen more closely to the story itself. What are the plot lines? How does the story itself unfold? And what makes it so compelling for today's culture?

Key ideas in this chapter

- Stories have the ability to grab people's attention, connect with their emotions, and open them up to the possibility of change. The change-makers of the sexual revolution understood this. They condensed complex intellectual arguments into memorable bite-size messages, and then wove them together into great stories.

- Biopics and dramas that portray heroic struggle appeal to today's individualistic way of moral thinking. By evoking empathy with their principal character, they draw out those moral instincts that care about individual needs, rather than those that appeal to the 'big' sacred values underpinning the welfare of the community as a whole.
- Much of the success of the sexual revolution can be attributed to its use of the entertainment industry as its main weapon of cultural subversion. But real-life stories of costly resistance and selfless compassion had a powerful impact in kindling people's individualistic moral reactions as well.
- Christians need to think hard before responding to culture change solely with more argument; they need more (and better) culture that tells its own stories. They must embody ways of life that show how their sacred values and convictions work to serve the needs of the many as well as the few.

5 THE NARRATIVE OF THE REVOLUTION

How the revolution hooked our inner hero and promised abundant life

> *Some of these things are true and some of them lies.*
> *But they are all good stories.*
> Hilary Mantel, *Wolf Hall*

So a good narrative tends to have a story-like trajectory: it portrays people and events and, usually, grapples with some kind of trouble that needs to be resolved. Before we try to unravel the narrative of the sexual revolution, however, let's clear up the difference between a narrative and a statement. Consider this sentence:

> The problem of human sin is resolved in the atoning death of Christ.

This is a statement rather than a narrative. It is a clear summary of one of the central truths of the Christian gospel, but there's no sense of context or action, no unexpected turn of events, and no sense of trajectory. Now consider this:

For God so loved the world that he gave his one and only Son, that whoever believes in him shall not perish but have eternal life.

Here is a narrative. It sets the scene with God's love for his world, encounters a problem of human 'perishing', and then, in the story of how God gives his own Son, provides a resolution. The narrative doesn't contain all the truth about the Christian gospel of course, but connects us with other storylines that will help to flesh it out.

With this in mind, what do you think the narrative of the sexual revolution looks like? I think it goes something like the one shown in the panel here:

> For centuries, traditional morality had us – all of us – in its suffocating grip. Year after year the same old rules, chained to the past, heaped shame on ordinary men and women (and boys and girls) whose only crime was being different. Enemies of the human spirit, these bankrupt ideologies befriended bigots and encouraged the spiteful. They nurtured a seedbed of hypocrisy and offered safe havens to perpetrators of abuse.
>
> No more. Change is here. We are breaking free from the shackles of bigotry and removing ourselves from under the dead hand of tradition. Our time has come. A time to be ourselves. A time to be truly who we are. A time to celebrate love wherever we find it. A time for the human spirit to flourish once again. And if you people won't move out of our way, we are going to push you out of our way.

Not bad, is it? It contains a clear and relatively simple message. It conveys ideas about what it means to be human ('just be who you are') and how humans flourish ('celebrate love wherever you find it'). It starts with trouble and it ends with a clear resolution. It conveys a sense of confidence and vision for the future. It connects with real stories involving real people. It makes possible a range of subordinate sound bites (e.g. 'what's wrong with two people just loving each other?'), and perhaps most importantly, its dramatic tension feeds into Hollywood scripts that our greatest actors can bring to life before our eyes.

There are three points in the above narrative that are crucial for conveying the revolution's key messages.

The narrative's heroic individualism

First, in this narrative the hero is *you*. This is all about finding your inner strength and being your own hero. Paul J. Zak (whom we met in the last chapter) suggests that the theme of *looking deep inside yourself* is the hallmark of all great heroic narrative:

> It starts with something new and surprising, and increases tension with difficulties that the characters must overcome, often because of some failure or crisis in their past, and then leads to a climax where the characters *must look deep inside themselves* [emphasis mine] to overcome the looming crisis, and once this transformation occurs, the story resolves itself.[1]

But is Zak right? Has the 'look-inside-yourself' motif been a defining characteristic of the heroic arc drama throughout human history? I don't think so. This is rather the hallmark of the modern hero. For example, contrast Zak's claim with the ancient story of David and Goliath. Here is the archetypal narrative of the giant slayer in which a young man takes on a military champion in single-handed combat against seemingly overwhelming odds. As author Malcolm Gladwell observes, by maintaining enough distance from his adversary to deploy his deadly sling-shot with lethal effect, David shows extraordinary cunning and tactical ability.[2]

But does David 'look inside himself' for help and deliverance? This is precisely the dramatic point of tension that sits at the heart of the story – on what, or rather on whom, will David rely to defeat the forces aligned against him? We read, 'The LORD who rescued me from the paw of the lion and the paw of the bear will rescue me from the hand of this Philistine' (1 Samuel 17:37).

And again: 'All those gathered here will know that it is not by sword or spear that the LORD saves; for the battle is the LORD's, and he will give all of you into our hands' (1 Samuel 17:47).

David repudiates his hero within. Instead, he puts his trust in another hero, one greater than himself: 'For the battle *is the* LORD'*s.*'

This story reminds us that in contrast to the revolution's narrative, the Christian faith is rooted in the repudiation of self-reliance: it is a far-reaching submission to a Hero bigger than 'me'. It's about being saved from sin. It's about self-denial. And yet the narrative of radical individualism is now so strong that after centuries of cultural dominance, this worldview appears repressive and harmful, and those who subscribe to it are made to feel strange.

The narrative's redemptive trajectory

Second, notice how the revolution's narrative draws you into its struggle for something better. As you read it, maybe the face of Alan Turing (portrayed by Benedict Cumberbatch) or Harvey Milk (Sean Penn) flickers at the back of your mind.

Or perhaps you see shamed young women put to work in Magdalene laundry asylums presided over by bitchy women dressed as nuns.

There are heroic strands here too, capturing something of the sense of struggle against the seemingly impossible odds of organized religion and political elites. There's heroic commitment, determination, the readiness for blood, sweat and tears, and a willingness to risk all for a greater good. Finally, there is the tension generated by the remaining forces of conservatism. The agents of religious repression may be cowed, but there is still more work to be done. Hence the call to keep up the fight: join in the struggle and discover the power of authenticity for yourself.

The narrative's claim to the moral high ground

Third, notice how the dominant narrative of the revolution makes an uncompromising claim to the moral high ground. In chapter 3, while exploring psychologist Jonathan Haidt's moral foundations theory, we observed how today's culture privileges the individualizing moral instincts found in moral systems one to three in the diagram. As a result, when we are faced with an ethical question, we tend to default to the moral intuitions at the left of the spectrum: 'Is anybody getting hurt here?' 'Is somebody being unfairly treated or oppressed?'

The revolution's narrative taps into these individualizing moral instincts and brings them to the top of the pack. It points to the harm of the 'suffocating grip' of tradition, and the oppression wrought by 'enemies of the human spirit . . . heaping shame on ordinary men and women'. There is a sense of moral crusade in the determination to get out from under the oppressive grip of tradition. It's all there, in just two short paragraphs.

Homecoming

I rest my case for the power of narrative with a video called *Homecoming*, readily available on YouTube.[3] Released around the time of the debate leading up to the introduction of gay marriage in the UK, this short film (100 seconds and shot on a remarkably low budget) quickly attracted over a million views, making it one of the most successful ads promoting gay marriage.[4]

In the lead-up to the vote in the UK Parliament, a prominent backer of gay marriage posted the video on Twitter, with the comment: 'This says it all for me.' But what does the film actually *say*? It portrays a British soldier returning home from Afghanistan on leave. As he descends from the air transporter on to the tarmac alongside his fellow soldiers, everybody else begins to peel away to greet wives and girlfriends. Children are hugged in happy reunions.

The soldier (let's call him 'Graham' for our purposes) looks around anxiously, searching the crowd. And then his face lights up in recognition. Another young man who has been standing, smiling among the waiting wives, starts to run (filmed in slow motion) towards him. As they embrace, he falls to his knees, pulls out a ring and proposes marriage.

The point is that this 100-second clip that 'says it all' actually *says* nothing – there are no words, just images. Images that convey powerful messages. Graham has been fighting to keep you safe, and you need to get on his side: he deserves a great homecoming. Moreover, he looks like the brother you wish you had or the nice young man every potential mother-in-law dreams of. As a fellow soldier embraces his own wife and children, you notice Graham's hand rising to pat him warmly on the back – a silent gesture of solidarity saying 'good for you'. And you, the viewer, find yourself asking, 'But what about you, Graham?' No longer a passive observer, your instincts for fairness have kicked in.

As Graham's eyes search the crowd, the narrative tension mounts, and yours with it – is there anybody out there? To his, and your, relief, another fine young man can now be observed running to greet him. Two beautiful young men in love. What can be wrong with that? The only words in the whole piece appear silently just before the credits roll:

All men can be heroes.
All men can be husbands.
End marriage discrimination.

Provided that you don't think about it, the logic appears impeccable. But that is the purpose – the pace of the narrative, enhanced by its emotionally resonant soundtrack, speeds you to the desired outcome: all men can be heroes; so all men can be husbands.

It's a no-brainer.

In the face of such artistry, orthodox Christians feel defeated. When I show some of this material in seminars and lectures, climaxing with *Homecoming*, ministers and lay people become visibly disheartened. One minister put up his hand and commented, 'Well, I hope the second half of your talk is going to be good, because if I'm honest, this is the narrative I think I believe.' The expressions on faces around the room signalled that he was not alone. It takes courage to put this sense of dis-ease into words. Even where Christians maintain an intellectual allegiance to orthodox teaching, years of watching TV and movies have captured hearts and emptied minds.

The odds seem overwhelming. What chance does an awkwardly structured thirty-minute sermon delivered once a week by an averagely gifted preacher have against such cultural power? What chance a fumbling talk about sex given by a red-faced father to a squirming eleven-year-old, set against the images and stories that have been tumbling across his screens for years. What chance a stilted 'relationships talk' for teenagers being herded off to some Christian camp? What chance that a young woman will unearth the courage to stand against the flow when she can already smell her pastor's silent fear?

No wonder that, as surveys show, a clear majority of the population are now in favour of gay marriage, and levels of support among Christians, including those happy to call themselves evangelical, are tracking upwards too.[5]

It's the heart, stupid!

For those who still believe that the biblical vision is good news, what is there to learn from the revolution's ability to bring about such far-reaching cultural change? It's the heart, stupid! Ironically, our secular culture seems to understand the biblical doctrine of the heart better than we do. Centuries ago the English Reformer Thomas Cranmer had a clearer insight: 'What the heart loves, the will chooses and the mind justifies.'[6]

Knowing nothing of the psychological evidence, Cranmer understood that the heart is the wanting, loving, seeking epicentre of the person. Our passions lead the way, and our thoughts follow. The elephant moves first.

Think about what satisfies you. What makes you tick? When we answer this question honestly, we are getting closer to what is really going on in our lives, because we *become what we love*. This view of being human means that if you want to change people, you need to change what they want, what they are prepared to worship. The thinkers and communicators of the sexual revolution understood this. They changed hearts by entertaining them. In compelling narratives they cast a vision of authenticity and freedom that made people say, 'That is what I want!'

In this chapter we have explored the pivotal role that the media and entertainment played in advancing the revolution's cause. But it would be folly to ignore the part played by the revolution's activists and campaigners. As we'll see, they too seemed to have a remarkable understanding of the human heart.

Key ideas in this chapter

- The core narrative of the sexual revolution has a broadly three-part structure: heroic individualism; a redemptive trajectory; a clear moral vision.
- This narrative connects strongly with ordinary people because of its appeal to the heart through the moral instincts of compassion and the defeat of oppression.
- Orthodox Christians must rediscover a narrative that appeals to the heart as well as the head. They will need to find a way of confronting the appeal of individualism while offering a convincing redemptive trajectory of their own.

6 THE WARRIORS OF THE REVOLUTION

How activists played a key role in making the revolution happen

> *Without Stonewall, change could never have happened*
> *so rapidly and so peacefully. The revolution won't be*
> *complete, until equality is accepted at home, at school,*
> *at work and in the streets. So we must continue*
> *to support Stonewall's essential initiatives,*
> *knowing right is on our side.*
> Ian McKellen[1]

The actor Ian McKellen, a leading LGBT rights advocate, makes a good point here. Without advocacy groups such as Stonewall, change would have come much more slowly. There's a chance it might not have happened at all.

Permanent revolution?

We should pay attention to McKellen's words on two counts. First, did you notice how this is a *moral crusade* being pursued by moral warriors? Once again we encounter the revolution's moral vision – it's about right and wrong, and there's no room for flexibility on this point. But then, second, notice how he says that it's not over yet. There is more to be done in terms of inclusion and equality. Progress has been spectacular, but there's more to come.

Given that they face the reality of ongoing campaigning, orthodox Christians need to pay closer attention to the insights, as well as the techniques, of advocacy groups and organizations. This isn't about disrespecting them – far from it. I'm not interested in the culture war mindset that asks only what we can learn from our opponents in order to defeat them. We need to build genuine bridges based on respect, even while acknowledging profound differences of worldview and morality. There are areas of common cause, like opposing bullying in schools and defending civil rights. But given the spectacular effectiveness and levels of funding of advocacy groups, Christians who want to preserve their identity and way of life need to pay close attention to the methods and tactics that will continue to be used against them for some time to come.

I am not saying that all this is being achieved in smoke-filled rooms where activists plot their way to power. But we must not be naive about the fact that advocacy groups and activists *do* think about strategy and tactics, often very carefully. Sasha Issenberg's book *The Victory Lab*[2] documents how political activists behind Obama's 2012 campaign for re-election were not afraid to use the tools of behavioural science. A self-styled consortium of behavioural scientists fed his campaign team a steady stream of ideas about how to portray their opponents in a negative light and mobilize wavering voters.[3]

So what techniques of persuasion are being used to accelerate the sexual revolution? And what should Christians learn from them?

Pay attention to your own community first, and change the world later

This book isn't about LGBT issues, but rather the broader unravelling of the Christian moral order that affects us all. Nevertheless, LGBT groups are especially skilled at advocacy and have built up a huge reservoir of experience. The main take-home lesson from their work is that if you want to survive as a minority, your first priority must be to maintain and support the convictions of your own members.

This happened in a number of different ways. They mobilized an impressive library of intellectual materials alongside more popular literature explaining their cause. Even more importantly, they nourished the confidence of their community through support groups, community centres and joint action committees. They were particularly good at providing attractive models of courage and persistence, and images of ways of life that evoke sympathy and admiration. In sum, they not only furnished their communities with intellectual ballast; they fired their imagination as well.

But activists knew that if they wanted to make progress beyond their own walls, they needed to become so confident in what they believed that it would *make them feel proud*. And so the Freedom marches of the early days of gay liberation became Gay Pride marches, and then transitioned to Pride Festivals and Pride Celebrations. Some of these festivals had all the atmosphere (well, almost) of a family day out. Gay activists understood that if you want your members to become ambassadors for minority beliefs, you must do more than simply believe – you must live what you believe in. And you must *put it on display*.

Pride. The flagrant sexual exhibitionism and provocative gesturing that marked (and still marks) some Gay Pride events leads many Christians to miss the point. These are not festivals of sexual debauchery. They are secular liturgies that placard people's deeply held convictions about what it means to be human and, in doing so, embed them further in the hearts and minds of those who hold them.

Having paid attention to strengthening their own community in this way, activists could then turn their attention to winning the argument in the public square. How did they set about doing that? The old 'good cop/bad cop' routine turned out to be as effective as ever.

Bad cop: ridicule your opponent

On a Sunday morning, 12 April 1998, Dr Carey, Archbishop of Canterbury, was delivering his traditional Easter sermon in Canterbury Cathedral. Suddenly he was dramatically interrupted by the British gay rights campaigner Peter Tatchell. There followed a disorderly brawl as the Archbishop stepped awkwardly aside in order to allow a senior police officer and stewards to drag the protesters out of the cathedral. The protesters scored a magnificent coup when a photograph of Tatchell clinging stubbornly to a huge stone pillar with stewards hammering at his hands appeared on the front pages of newspapers the next day. It sat rather awkwardly alongside the Archbishop's sermon urging peace in Northern Ireland.[4]

Do you see what happened here? The Archbishop was made to look ridiculous. Turn up a manual for political activists and there it is – one of the cardinal rules: 'Ridicule is your best and most potent weapon.'[5]

Bad cop: shame your opponent

Tatchell's words were actually even more important that day than his actions:

> Dr Carey supports discrimination against lesbian and gay people. He opposes lesbian and gay human rights. This is not a Christian teaching. It is wrong for Dr Carey to oppose an equal age of consent.

Once again notice the moral force of the argument. This is about right denouncing wrong. Tatchell's intervention has all the appearance of an Old Testament prophet calling down God's judgment. Carey is accused of lacking compassion ('he doesn't care about children fostered by gay people who would be deprived of a home'); disregarding fairness and equality ('he supports discrimination'); and oppressing those with whom he disagrees ('he opposes equal opportunities for lesbian and gay people at work'). In just a few simple slogans Tatchell wields all three of Jonathan Haidt's individualizing moral systems of compassion, fairness and freedom from oppression. Carey has been weighed in the balance and found wanting. He stands in shame. And in the blaze of publicity that followed, ordinary Christians took careful note. Next time this could be me . . .

The return of shame

Author Andy Crouch believes that Western individualism is triggering a new kind of shame culture, or what he terms 'fame-shame' culture:

> [In today's individualistic culture that has weakened links to family and institutions fame is bestowed by a broad audience,

with only the loosest bonds to those they acclaim] . . .
Because fame-oriented culture lacks the traditional structures
of community and honor, those in it dread being excluded
or shamed . . . In fame-shame culture, people yearn to feel
included in the group, a state constantly endangered, fragile,
and desperately in need of protection.[6]

Crouch's insight is that Western individualism has loosened
the social ties that help to protect people from 'loss of face'
in other cultures. Because of more socially fragmented ways
of life, families and friends no longer pull together to support
each other in the same way. And so, in a social media world,
we have to manage our reputations before a much broader,
less connected Facebook public with powerful tools for
evoking humiliation and shame. And when the mob turns
against you, there isn't much to buffer its power to shame.
    Here's Crouch again:

Kara Powell, executive director of the Fuller Youth Institute,
recalls a moment of shame from her adolescence. 'There
were maybe five kids sitting in a car across the street,' she
says, recounting how she tripped and fell. 'I remember them
laughing at me as I picked myself up. But that was in front
of five kids, and it was over in five minutes. Today, if someone
caught a moment like that on a smartphone and shared it
on social media, that shame could live with the kid for the
rest of high school.'[7]

Activists have capitalized on the fame-shame culture of
Western individualism. In effect, the public pillory has returned
in virtual form, with frightening effectiveness. A few days ago
a friend recounted an incident in which his teenage daughter
had voiced her opposition, on the grounds of her Christian

convictions, to the then recent introduction of 'gay marriage'. Over the next few days she watched with horror as, one by one, her Facebook contacts quietly 'unfriended' her.

The result of this emotional exclusion is that orthodox Christians, who may be quite happy to make known their views on animal rights, politics and just about any other topic you care to mention, have learned to excise any reference to sex, marriage and the family from their social media profile. They have joined their leaders in the Great Silence.

Good cop: offer your opponent a way out

Let's return to the good cop/bad cop scenario. It's time for the bad cop to make his exit: with one last threat and a dramatic flourish, the bad cop storms out of the room, appalled by your naked resistance and stubborn denial. You remain alone, afraid, isolated and ashamed. The price you are being asked to pay may simply be too high, and you are looking for a way out.

Enter the good cop. That is precisely what he is going to offer you. A way out. The dynamics mean that you cannot, and will not, concede the case to your cruel assailant who has wisely left the room. If you can be so easily bullied and threatened out of your convictions, then what were they worth in the first place? Few people are willing to concede that their convictions and beliefs were based on such a house of cards. A face-saving formula is required. That is what the good cop is here for.

In contrast to the bad cop, the good cop appears sympathetic and kind. He tries to create an emotional connection with you by expressing dislike for the bad cop as well. He doesn't agree with his methods and he wants to make this as easy for you as he can. So he hopes you will be able to cooperate so that neither of you will have to deal with him again and this whole unpleasant business can be resolved.

In a criminal scenario this may simply require a straight-forward admission of guilt. But in the case of the sexual revolution, the good cop has to work harder: we are socially righteous creatures who want to be seen, and need to be seen, to be doing the 'right thing'. So suppose the good cop offers you a way out of this, which involves just that – doing the *right* thing? What if the change of heart he is seeking doesn't involve so much a disloyal capitulation from you as a bold exercise of moral courage?

Now you are confused because there is moral force in his argument. And because you live in the relative silence of your religious minority group, you have few apologetic resources to rebut it. And so, just like the grandmother in chapter 3, you do a slide along the moral systems spectrum from the right to the left by replacing the old moral instincts of loyalty to sacred convictions with the more socially acceptable and emotionally rewarding instincts of compassion and fairness. And if you are of a youthful and rebellious disposition, it furnishes the added righteous bonus of appearing to swim against the tide. So now a defection is less a weak-minded betrayal and more a defiant act of moral courage.

Before I draw this together in terms of its impact on the contemporary church, I need to repeat that most activists are motivated to convince other people, using every means in their power, because they believe they are fighting for something that is good and true. They believe in what they are doing, often with a depth of conviction and personal sacrifice beyond anything seen among those they oppose.

But regardless of motives, the effects on Christian communities of this relentless activism have been dramatic and far-reaching. They are the casualties of the revolution. So with more to come, is it time to throw in the towel? Is it really possible to resist the ongoing campaign? These are potent challenges. Which is why, in the next chapter, I'm going to try to convince you that if orthodox Christians want to survive as a minority in today's culture, they need to start acting like one.

Key ideas in this chapter

- Activists and advocacy organizations have played an important role in the success of the sexual revolution, sometimes using insights from the social sciences to develop techniques of persuasion.
- Advocacy groups paid careful attention to building a sense of pride and ownership of their beliefs within their own communities. This not only sustained their convictions in the face of opposition, but also underpinned the development of authentic stories of what this way of life can actually look like.
- The new shame culture of social media offered added traction to the ability of activists to portray their opponents as morally deficient. At the same time they offered a strong moral alternative as a face-saving formula for falling into line.
- As these activities are likely to continue, orthodox Christians need to think about how to strengthen their own beliefs and the cohesion of their own communities. They could start by learning from the activists who have opposed them so successfully.

7 THE CASUALTIES OF THE REVOLUTION

Why surviving as a minority means you need to start acting like one

Imagine you are taking part in a psychological experiment. You have been seated at the end of a row of ten people. Each person in line has been tasked with estimating which of three lines on a card placed a few metres away is the closest in length to a line drawn on a second card that sits beside it.

At first sight the task looks pretty simple and straightforward – clearly the correct answer is line number two. As people further up the line start to announce their results, however, to your surprise everybody else is choosing line number one. This is clearly wrong, but you are in a *cognitive minority* – that is, you hold a belief about the world that is different from everybody else around you.

How likely is it that you would stick to your guns and give the correct answer?

It was the sociologist Peter Berger who first used the term 'cognitive minorities' to describe those whose views about the world differed significantly from the mainstream of their surrounding culture.[1] Think of Muslims. Or Orthodox Hasidic Jews. Berger contends that, given intense social and psychological pressures to conform, if you want to survive as a cognitive minority, you must take active steps to safeguard and nurture your beliefs. In other words, to survive as a minority you need to start acting like one.

Christians have occupied the cultural mainstream for so long that we find the idea of being a minority difficult to stomach, never mind the thought of acting like one. But we need to make the adjustment, and soon, because, in addition to having become a cognitive minority, we are now also viewed as an *immoral minority*. In other words, as well as having different beliefs from everybody else, we are now frequently cast as having inferior morals. This puts us in a social and psychological space that is fraught with danger.

So our journey of understanding faces one last task. We need to explore the lived experience of cognitive and moral minorities, and especially those that have not yet come to terms with their status. What happens inside their communities? Who are the casualties? What do they need to do in order to survive?

Human beings are dangerous conformists

Let's return to our psychological laboratory. As the line experiment continues, and people further up the line continue to announce their (wrong) answers, what will you say? I suspect the vast majority of my readers are absolutely confident that they would stick with their correct answer. But in a real-life experiment what would you *actually* do?

The scenario I have just described is one of the most famous experiments in the history of psychology. It was carried out by Solomon Asch back in 1950.[2] Although the subject thinks that he (or she) is just one in a row of other volunteer subjects, in fact he is the only *real* subject, the stooge of the experiment. All the remaining 'subjects' are actually confederates of the experimenter. And they have been primed to give wrong answers.

So what happened in Asch's experiments? Three-quarters of the stooge subjects gave the wrong answer on at least one occasion, and more than a third gave the wrong answer for more than half the time. All-female groups tended to conform significantly more often than all-male groups. You can watch a video of similar experiments on this website.[3]

When the stooge subjects were later asked about their motives, some appeared genuinely to believe that their (incorrect) answer had been the correct one; others were confident that the rest of the group were wrong but didn't want to say so ('Why should I make waves?'). Levels of conformity with confederates dropped dramatically if subjects were given a 'partner' alongside, primed to agree with them, but then rose again if the partner was suddenly called out of the room.

The point about these experiments is that it's hard to swim against the flow. Of course we all know this. But we think it applies to everybody else. In fact, we are *all* susceptible, and the greater the costs of non-conforming, the more likely it is that you will fall in line. Asch's work demonstrates how difficult it is for human beings to stick out from the crowd. We hate being the odd one out. Holding views that are dissonant from the majority makes us feel uncomfortable, excluded, distrusted. It puts us under the uncomfortable spotlight of other people's scrutiny. So we hide what we really think or, when forced to express our view, we search for possible reasons to change our mind.

Many ideas are simply taken on trust, depending on the social support they receive

One way to resist the pressure is to band together into the kind of 'cognitive minority' group I mentioned above. As we saw in chapter 2, sociologist Peter Berger, who coined the term, has been especially interested in exploring the link between ideas and the social support they receive. If you want to keep your ideas alive, Berger argues, you need to make sure that they are actively nurtured and sustained in your particular social setting. They have to be made plausible to group members, otherwise they won't survive.

Let's dig a little further into this link between ideas and their social setting. Everybody holds ideas about the world which they haven't examined or questioned properly. Much of what we believe we take on trust – because others (particularly the kind of people we tend to trust) say so. Take the theory of evolution. Beyond general notions of survival of the fittest, most people who say they believe in evolution have little detailed scientific data to hand that would give real evidential substance to their belief. They take it on trust.

Berger coined the term 'plausibility structures' to describe the social processes that encourage us to take ideas on trust. For example, an idea's plausibility is strengthened when it is heard frequently in the media, or advanced by attractive role models whom we respect or by intellectual elites who seem to know what they are talking about. The most powerful plausibility structure is the tone we adopt when ideas are exchanged in conversation: it is hard to resist a tone of voice that implies 'everybody knows this', particularly when it is accompanied by nodding heads around the table. Once an idea is assumed to be true in the 'conversational fabric' of a society, that idea has pretty much made it.

Take the case of a young mum who holds conservative views on sex and marriage. She happens to say something to a friend about her daughter one day 'meeting the right man'. 'Or the right woman,' her friend interjects quickly. 'We want our daughter to know that it doesn't matter who you marry as long as the two people love each other.' This view isn't offered as one among many, but in a tone that suggests it's the only show in town. The intonation alone conveys the inference that 'all right-minded people think this today, don't they?' This adds powerful plausibility, and makes the idea hard to resist.

If a cognitive minority wants to survive, it needs to start acting like one

Because of the strength of the plausibility structures support-ing the majority views in a society, if you have ideas different from everybody else, it is generally a good plan to be part of a support network. As we learned from Asch's experiments, even one compatriot with a view similar to yours strengthens your hand. Kindred spirits are crucial to keeping minority ideas alive. And so cognitive minority groups, if they want to survive as a minority, must start to act like a minority. They need to make active efforts to nourish their beliefs and patterns of life in ways that make them plausible to their members. They need intellectual leaders, attractive role models and the opportunity for members to rehearse and consolidate their ideas in the conversational fabric of their group, just like the majority outside.

But what happens if there is no leadership or modelling of beliefs, or little that makes them seem plausible? Berger said that the minority is effectively doomed. The organizers of Gay Pride understood this. But where is the confidence, let alone a sense of pride, in the contemporary church's posture towards issues of sex and relationships? The danger is heightened by the fact that Christian beliefs are frequently viewed as morally dangerous and antithetical to human well-being. Indeed, some contend that these beliefs cause harm.

Under these pressures, people's convictions come under severe strain. The first people to leach out of the minority are those with more empathic personality types. They *feel* the emotional exclusion more strongly. Those that remain tend to be more 'black-and-white' personality types, who also tend to circle the wagons around authoritarian figures. This alienates any remaining empathic types further, so that eventually, as they continue to leave, the minority effectively becomes an authoritarian rump, or simply implodes.

Double jeopardy of shame

These dynamics expose orthodox Christians to a double jeopardy of shame. Take the case of a sixteen-year-old boy brought up in a Christian home trying hard to stay connected with faith in a small youth group containing few other boys. He is outgoing, relational and sporty. The other boys in his group are socially awkward, bookish and reserved.

In contrast to his feelings at church, at school he feels relaxed among his sporting friends. Except in the area of sex. And there's a lot of it in the air. When friends talk about some seedy porn, or what happened at a party the night before, his awkward silence makes *him* look creepy. And he's more than aware of what people think about the bigotry of religion. The result is a deepening sense of shame and exclusion.

In fact, our teenager faces a double jeopardy of shame. He experiences shame outside *and* inside the church. The legacy of Greek philosophy (and remnants of Gnosticism) means that the vast majority of Christians have entered the experience of being made sexual in ignorance and fear. In shame. In the oft-quoted words of Don Schrader: 'To hear many religious people talk, one would think God created the torso, head, legs and arms, but the devil slapped on the genitals.' And that is what many Christians still *feel*.

As an eight- or nine-year-old boy, I once asked my grandmother what the word 'pregnant' meant. Of course I had a good idea, but it sounded naughty and I wanted to see what she would say. She denied all knowledge of the word, but her evasiveness gave the game away. Eventually, the truth was outed, but her flushed appearance enveloped the whole interaction in a cloud of shame. You can imagine what the remainder of my sex education was like.

Young people today do better than this. But often not much better. Many still stumble into the awareness of their sexuality through the prism of what the church is against rather than what it is for. I am frequently invited to give a talk on the question of pornography. Almost always I decline unless it forms part of a positive body of teaching on the biblical vision for sex. I am no longer prepared to help perpetuate a culture that knows what it is *against*, but has little idea about what it is *for*. The resulting double jeopardy of shame provokes an intolerable level of dissonance for the human spirit, and young people continue to quietly plot their exit strategy as I write.

OK, let's keep a sense of proportion here. Churches that hold to orthodox teaching on sex and relationships are not yet losing *huge* numbers of teenagers and young people. Indeed, compared with more liberal church traditions where the situation is dire, the future looks relatively bright. But we are losing the silent revolution that is taking place in their hearts. And at some point something will give.

So as we stand among children, teenagers and young adults in our churches who are silently struggling with these issues, we're at a good point to take stock of where we now go. What does the future hold for them? What does it hold for us?

In this first part of the book we have aimed to understand the sexual revolution in terms of its ideology, its moral claims and the power it possesses through narrative to win hearts and minds. Armed with these insights, how should we now respond?

How should we respond?

Three tasks lie ahead.

A better critique

First, orthodox Christians need a better critique of the revolution. We need to connect more skilfully and thoughtfully with minds and hearts already won over by the revolution's ideology and moral vision. This is the burden of Christian apologetics, as the apostle Paul demonstrated in his famous address to the Athenian pagans on Mars Hill. Paul proclaimed Christ and the resurrection, yes. But he also worked hard to look at the world through the eyes of his listeners, to identify common ground where possible and win a hearing. And so too must we.

There are important matters of tone and relationship that need attention. This involves listening, really listening, to our opponents. There needs to be some heart-searching about the past too. Where there has been prejudice, hatred even, this needs to be recognized in real repentance. Not all churches or individual Christians acted in this way, far from it. But some have, and we should be ready to own up. The first test of genuine, gospel engagement is to look into our hearts to examine our motives: do we want to win people or win arguments? Do we try to practise what we preach? Do people encounter our vision in who we are and how we live, as well as in what we say?

A good conversation starts by looking for the common ground. As we listen to those with whom we disagree, we should be ready to recognize compassion where we find it and respect the logic behind some of the arguments being made. What goals do we share with our opponent? Often you will discover that you both believe in freedom; you both believe that the individual is important; you both want to see people flourish. Of course there are huge differences over what these words mean and how we achieve these transcendent goals. But wherever we encounter the desire for human flourishing, let's recognize our opponents' humanity and lay claim to that ground as well.

Finally, we shouldn't begin our critique of the revolution in terms of *what we believe*, but, crucially, *in terms of what it promised*. We need to examine the revolution on the basis of the vision it offered and the outcomes that it promised. Is it delivering the freedom, flourishing and well-being that it assured us? In the shadow of the revolution, is everybody really living happily ever after? We'll investigate these questions in the second part of this book by marshalling evidence from the social sciences and popular culture.

A better story

Second, as we have seen already, we cannot engage with a great narrative by deploying more facts. We have to tell a different story. A better story. We must out-narrate those with whom we disagree. We shouldn't use narrative as a cynical debating device to outwit our opponents and win the argument. We need to tell stories because this is how the human mind works, and because Jesus himself paved the way with some of the greatest stories ever told. Stories of acceptance and inclusion in the gospel's call to repentance, stories of brokenness restored and lives reshaped.

Better storytellers

Third and finally, we must learn how to be better storytellers. Our story needs to be rooted in our deepest conviction and made real and plausible in our own lives and those of our communities. There is nothing more powerful than a story told with conviction out of the flesh-and-blood reality of your own experience. And we need artists as well as artisans, investing in new media and the imaginative use of the visual arts. This is the proclamation of the whole gospel, the gospel of God's grace, the gospel that says Jesus Christ has reconciled *all* things – minds, hearts and our most intimate sexual longing – to himself. So in part 2 we begin by asking, how can Christians begin to offer a better critique?

Key ideas in this chapter

- Human beings are dangerous conformists who find it hard to swim against the flow. The experience of being an immoral, as well as a cognitive, minority creates an overwhelming social pressure to conform.
- The most vulnerable individuals are the more empathic and those whose views are less well formed intellectually. Cognitive minorities who fail actively to sustain and nurture the plausibility of their ideas put their members at serious risk. Those individuals who are most empathic will be the first to depart, leaving a remnant inclined to 'black-and-white' thinking and authoritarian diktat.

- In today's culture Christians face a double jeopardy
  of shame from their own internal shame structures
  and their experience as an immoral minority in wider
  society. Young people are especially susceptible and
  are likely to vote with their feet.
- These dynamics underscore the need for orthodox
  Christians to begin to act like a minority. Convictions
  and distinctive modes of life must be actively nurtured
  and sustained. This involves empathic opinion leaders
  capable of winning hearts and minds in a robust defence
  of their convictions. It also requires that minority beliefs
  are made plausible and real in the lived experience of
  creative and internally supportive communities.

Part 2

A BETTER CRITIQUE

8 THE PLANK IN YOUR OWN EYE

A Christian critique of the sexual revolution must begin with honest self-examination

> How can you say to your brother, 'Let me take the speck out of your eye,' when all the time there is a plank in your own eye? You hypocrite, first take the plank out of your own eye, and then you will see clearly to remove the speck from your brother's eye.
> (Matthew 7:4–5)

Jesus' words are uncompromising and hard-hitting and leave us with no choice. A better critique of the sexual revolution must start with a better critique of ourselves.

This needs more than a grudging recognition that critics may have the occasional point here. The history of the church in the sphere of human sexuality is disfigured by shame and hypocrisy. Christendom's dysfunctional attitudes to sex helped create the discontent that triggered the revolution and propelled it forwards. And even though, as we shall see, the promise of the sexual revolution as an alternative has failed spectacularly, we need to recognize that *the promise itself* was for something better, more inclusive and life-giving than what we offered in the past. So it's time to face up to the shame, hypocrisy and prejudice that have discoloured our own Christian story and take it on the chin.

Facing up to shame

In the previous chapter I talked about the double jeopardy of shame affecting young people trying to hold to orthodox Christian teaching. Shame is the emotion of inferiority. We do not *think* shame; it rushes into our feelings unbeckoned and unwelcome. Shame leaves us feeling diminished, emotionally discoloured and excluded. For some, the experience is so powerful that their face goes red, they avoid eye contact, or they want to leave the room and hide.

Shame is the uninvited but ever-present companion of sexual desire. Do you remember how it felt when a parent attempted their first awkward stab at sex education with you: the excruciating conflict of wanting to know more while willing them to shut up? Some parents do a masterly job, but many Christian youngsters are simply offered a book, sent to some talk or exposed to an awkward lecture about the dangers (STIs etc.) of sex. The ability of shame to put a gag on parent–child interactions about sex means that for the vast majority of young people, social media and the school playground fill in the gaps.

Sex education in the secular sphere, and in schools, fares no better. One seventeen-year-old characterized his school-based sex education like this:

> The [school] sex education we got was like something
> from another age. We were told in class what a vulva
> was when I was 14, but by that time I had been inspecting

them in detail on my computer screen for years, and so had every other lad in the room. I knew what they looked like; what I didn't know was that there was such a huge emotional gap between porn and reality. That's what they need to teach.[1]

The reference to computer screens is the only clue to the fact that this is 2015 and not 1959. When parents do attempt to do their duty as sex educators, their efforts usually trail in the wake of the information already gleaned from elsewhere – peers, school, and of course the Internet. And even when they think they've made a reasonable stab at it, parents' self-assessments tend to differ wildly from their children's perceptions of what took place: in one survey, while 72 per cent of mothers 'strongly agreed' that they had talked with their adolescent children about sex, only 45 per cent of the young people involved concurred. Shame distorts perceptions on all sides of this tricky equation.[2]

Shame and human fallenness

Where does shame originate? In the creation accounts of Genesis shame was not part of the original divine mandate. Humans were created to be fruitful, and God declared their sexual fruitfulness 'very good'. In fact, the text states quite clearly (immediately after the verse about Adam and Eve being 'one flesh') that the man and his wife were both naked 'and . . . felt no shame' (Genesis 2:25). Paradise was a space in which everybody and everything was at home. Humans were at home in their world, at home in their own bodies, and at home with each other.

Until it all fell apart. As the repercussions of that first terrible act of human disobedience began to ripple outwards, they were witnessed first, and most noticeably, in Adam and Eve's body language. Everything was so out of place, so unnatural, so utterly *wrong*; they reacted by trying to hide.

Even before Adam and Eve's ridiculous attempt to hide from God, the effects of the fall were already unfolding with such force and speed that their first instinct was to hide from each other. Could they trust each other any more? Could they be sure their bodies were something that their partners loved and cherished? Or were their bodies now something the other simply *wanted*?

And so, even before Adam shamefully tries to pin the blame on his wife ('the woman you put here with me', Genesis 3:12), their sense of mutual suspicion so overwhelmed them that the body parts of their 'one-fleshness' had to be covered over with a girdle of fig leaves. They needed to put something between them – literally.

The result is that this side of the new heavens and new earth (Revelation 21:1), to some degree at least, feelings of shame will always discolour our experience of being sexual. Indeed, there are some areas in which shame provokes us to act *appropriately* in a fallen world where trust is in short supply. We can no longer open ourselves naively to other people's potentially lustful gaze, so there needs to be a proper sense of modesty and privacy about our bodies, particularly our intimate sexual characteristics. Modesty demands that this part of our bodies, this sphere of our 'one-fleshness', has a special status and meaning and is not available to just anybody and everybody. You can't really trust them with it.

But shame causes us to act *inappropriately* when we deny or repress our sexuality altogether. Or when it tells us that our sexuality simply doesn't belong in the story of our redemption. Or when it fuels the ugly relationship dynamics of blame and exclusion that led Adam to pin it all on the wife he loved. And if the sexual revolution has forced us to face up to this unwelcome intruder in our midst, then we should say 'thank you'. And mean it.

Hypocrisy

Mention the words 'hypocrisy' and 'church' in the same sentence, and shocking revelations of sexual abuse spring to mind. Where the sexual revolution has insisted we shine lights into the dark corners of our subculture, we should welcome its contribution. I am not convinced, however, by claims of a specific causal link between religion and sexual abuse. Revelations of large-scale abuse in the entertainment industry, the BBC, politics and education have put paid to the notion that Christian morality itself institutionalizes the conditions that make sexual abuse more likely.

But religious institutions *have* harboured the same evils as elsewhere. Worse, as the film *Spotlight* demonstrates, their internal structures, especially certain kinds of clericalism, have sustained some of the most harrowing examples of cover-up. So, regardless of the rampant hypocrisy we could expose among those at the epicentre of the sexual revolution itself, let's begin by freely acknowledging our own.

Another area of rank hypocrisy among traditionalist Christians has been the reality gap between convictions and behaviour, between the standards we impose on others and those we are willing to accept for ourselves. For example, Princeton sociologist Robert Wuthnow reports that among the young unmarried in the US, evangelical Protestants are most likely (about 42 per cent) to say that premarital sex is *always wrong*. And yet in the same survey, 69 per cent of unmarried evangelicals aged twenty-one to forty-five also report having had sex with at least one partner in the past year. How do you square that particular circle?[3]

Think about divorce in Christian communities too. On the face of it, divorce rates among evangelicals in the US have simply tracked those of secular culture. Indeed, one survey carried out by the Barna research centre in 2007 / 2008 reported that divorce rates among 'born-again' Christians were indistinguishable from those of other groups.[4] An earlier Barna report suggested that they may be even higher than those found among atheists and agnostics.

But how reliable are these kinds of data? Before we get too carried away, we need a little more fact-checking. On closer inspection, rates of divorce do indeed appear to be high among 'conservative Protestants' in the US, but 'nominal' conservative Christians who rarely go to church probably account for these higher rates.[5] In fact, divorce rates among regular attenders at places of worship (as opposed to nominal adherents) tend to be lower compared with secular Americans.[6]

The US phenomenon of nominal or cultural evangelicalism does not translate well into a European setting, so we do not know the true state of affairs among evangelicals in the UK. Nevertheless, at an anecdotal level, there are numerous examples of separation and divorce among UK Christians who hold otherwise orthodox views on sexual morality. Of course, there are circumstances where a separation is right and just, particularly where relationships have become abusive. But in other cases are we simply tracking the 'follow-your-own-dream' philosophy of our culture? We need to take criticism on the chin and address this large and unsightly plank in our own eye. And where the sexual revolution exposed our hypocrisy, once again, we should say 'thank you' – and mean it.

Fear, prejudice and disgust

Christian author Ed Shaw, speaking out of his own experience of same-sex attraction, documents the 'mis-steps' that disfigure communities of Christians around issues of human sexuality. In one section he puts his finger upon their tendency to elevate the sins associated with same-sex attraction above other sins, and particularly other types of 'sexual sin':

> So, do you want to make sexual godliness seem plausible to people like me? [Then] take Christlikeness seriously in every area of your life . . . don't demand of me anything that you are unwilling to demand of yourself. And when I have to confess my sexual sins to you, don't be afraid to confess your sexual sins to me.[7]

Ed counsels, 'Don't be afraid.' But we are afraid. Afraid of the reality that, in the image of God, we have been made sexual. Afraid of our shame. Afraid of our secrets.

I recently had the opportunity to interview, publicly, somebody who had faced the challenge of reconciling his same-sex attraction with his orthodox Christian convictions. The audience listened intently and offered a warm and heartfelt round of applause at the end. But I was uncomfortable about our applause. I found myself wondering how many of the rest of us would have been happy to be interviewed publicly about our own sexual desires and fantasies. I frequently encounter young single Christians who seem reluctant even to acknowledge that they have sexual attraction ('don't want to appear desperate!'). How many of them, in exchange for a round of applause, would be happy to step up and talk about their own sexual longings? How many in that audience struggling with pornography would have been willing to be interviewed about it? And yet, as Ed Shaw points out, we make demands upon those who are same-sex attracted that we would never ask of others.

Let's be clear, I am not arguing here that we should be more ready to talk about our personal journeys in public. I'm making the opposite point that an excessive public focus upon those who struggle with today's 'hot-button' issues can be a device for keeping our own struggles about being made sexual in the closet. When this happens, we are using other people's stories to hide our own, and the shame that goes with them. The answer isn't to start sharing personal matters publicly, but we do need to be ready to be more open about our struggles, to confront our shame, and to seek the right kind of pastoral care and discipline.

Orthodox Christians who voice their views in the public square are often unfairly and emotively accused of 'bigotry'; it is an easy way to close down debate and demean one's opponent. But where beliefs are grounded in emotion, rather than reasoned analysis, some orthodox Christians do display bigotry. Why do you think traditionalist Christians, like our grandmother in chapter 3, can change their convictions, sometimes at lightning speed, when a daughter or nephew or a godson 'comes out' as same-sex attracted? It is because they do an emotional 'flip', exchanging one emotional reaction for another. Pastor and church leader Timothy Keller makes a similar point:

And when I see people discarding their older beliefs that homosexuality is sinful after engaging with loving, wise, gay people, I'm inclined to agree that those earlier views were likely defective. In fact, they must have been essentially a form of bigotry. They could not have been based on theological or ethical principles, or on an understanding of historical biblical teaching. They must have been grounded instead on a stereotype of gay people as worse sinners than others (which is itself a shallow theology of sin). So I say good riddance to bigotry.[8]

He is surely right in this analysis. Shame is the cradle of bigotry because it propels us to project our disgust towards ourselves on to others. Orthodox convictions around sexual ethics need to be based in reason and calm analysis, not elephant-based gut responses driven by fear and disgust.

Which brings me back to my central point. The sexual revolution isn't primarily about the 'hot-button' issues being fiercely contested in the so-called culture wars. It is about a much wider, deeper unravelling. And where the revolution forces us to sit up and think, we should be grateful. There can be no 'going-backery'. No hankering after some bucolic paradise of the 1950s that never actually existed. Where the revolution has forced us to face our shame and hypocrisy, we should say 'thank you' – and mean it. Only then will we be ready to put the claims and promises of the sexual revolution under a critical spotlight.

Key ideas in this chapter

- A Christian response to the sexual revolution needs to begin with honest self-examination. The fear and shame that has marked much Christian culture in the area of sex and relationships isn't just harmful and repressive, it is unbiblical. And these attitudes, in part, helped lay the foundations of the revolution.
- Orthodox Christians often draw a line in the sand at the so-called hot-button moral issues (such as same-sex attraction) while turning a blind eye to bigger problems

of divorce and separation and the prevalence of sex outside marriage in their own ranks.

- We need to be sensitive to our motives when we critique the sexual revolution, and ensure that our moral stance is grounded in a clear understanding of the biblical narrative rather than gut reactions fuelled by shame and fear.
- There can be no 'going-backery' to some bucolic paradise of the 1950s that never actually existed. The sexual revolution is forcing us to rethink our grasp of the biblical moral vision. It is an opportunity rather than a problem, and we should be ready to seize it.

9 SLEEPING WITH THE ENEMY

The revolution promised more and better sex, but failed to deliver

Having acknowledged our own failures, we are in better shape to take a long, hard look at the failed promises of the revolution. When we critique the revolution on its terms rather than our own, what do we find? Are we all living happily ever after? Or have we been sleeping with the enemy?

Before we start, I need to acknowledge that in speaking of the 'sexual revolution' so broadly, I may be accused of setting up a series of straw men. In other words, I have misrepresented and caricatured the revolution in order to make it easier to attack. My argument, however, is with the revolution *as it is held in the popular imagination.* You may protest that your beliefs about sex have nothing to do with the core ideologies of the sexual revolution and its popular cultural narrative.[1] Nevertheless, this is the narrative driving the shifts in culture that we are witnessing today – in family life, communities and the welfare of children – and I make no apology for taking a hard-nosed look into what it is actually delivering.

So where should we begin?

Let's start with people's sex lives. What is really going on?

The promise of sexual liberation: more and better sex?

Set free from the shackles of shame imposed by religious tradition, the revolution promised that we would enjoy better sex. Sexual liberation isn't just about freedom from the dead hand of tradition – it's about freedom for sex, more and better sex. But did it deliver?

Oxford statistician David Spiegelhalter has written an authoritative, easy-to-digest guide to what we know about people's sex lives today. He is careful to emphasize the pitfalls and bear traps that lie in wait when we attempt to measure sexual attitudes and activities.[2] It's a sobering guide to the wildly inaccurate claims that circulate (especially in church circles) under the imprimatur: 'as science now tells us'. So with this in mind, and drawing on Spiegelhalter's work, what's really going on behind the curtains?

Spiegelhalter draws together convincing data that rather than decanting us into a sexual paradise of 'free love', the frequency of 'having sex' (defined as vaginal, oral or anal intercourse) has actually declined in recent years. And the trend is firmly downwards. Tongue-in-cheek, Spiegelhalter observes,

> At [this] rate of decline . . . a simple, but extremely naive, extrapolation would predict that by 2040 the average person will not be having any sex at all. I rather suspect this will not be the case, but this still leaves the crucial question: why is there less sex going on?[3]

These data sit at odds with breathless media reporting about some of today's sexual goings-on. According to one recent newspaper report, for example, gyms in the UK have become major 'hook-up' venues, where '25 per cent [of those polled] claimed to have had sex . . . at least once in the last 12 months'.[4] Really? Apparently 10 per cent of those attending gyms now pop a condom into their kit, 'just in case'. I must have been going along to my local gym with my eyes closed. 'Hook-up' apps create a similar impression. Tinder boasts that it 'sees 750 million swipes [how you can accept or reject a potential person of interest] and 10 million matches daily, with the average user spending a massive 77 minutes sorting out possible dates every day'.[5] Phew. Everybody is at it. But who to believe?

I'm with Spiegelhalter's analysis of the data.

Nobody knows why people are having less sex today. One idea is that people prefer staring at their iPads, computers and mobile surfing devices to looking at each other. Maybe the sheer number of options and competing demands on our time mean that sex just keeps falling down our list of priorities. Maybe. But whatever the cause, I think we can conclude that the revolution's promise of more sex is not being delivered.

We may be having less sex, but are we having better sex? Apparently not. Comparing the results of a sex survey carried out in 2008, and then repeated in 2014, a British newspaper headline recently warned, 'The nation has lost some of its sexual swagger.' Worrying over the 'declining national libido' and a 'collective lack of satisfaction', one commentator observed:

Before [the] age of austerity the average British adult enjoyed sex nearly seven times a month; in 2014 that figure has apparently double-dipped to a miserly four times – less than once a week – with a full third of the population admitting to no sex at all in those 30 days and nights . . . the nation's male population in particular appears to have lost a significant amount of horizontal confidence . . . the average British man's approval of the size of his manhood has drooped somewhat alarmingly over the last decade.[6]

Let's not get carried away with the rhetoric here. The article is based on a simple comparison of two cross-sectional on-line surveys involving a little over 1,000 people. Despite the pollster's efforts to gain a representative sample, these data are subject to all kinds of known and unknown biases. But although the jury may still be out on this one, there is certainly no evidence that the quality of people's sex lives is actually getting better.

All this leaves me wondering whether the vision of sexual liberation, supposedly set free from its broader Christian narrative of commitment and responsibility, simply doesn't have enough 'beef', enough intrinsic meaning and purpose, to motivate and sustain sexual interest over the longer term. In other words, the bravado of the sexual revolution, with its clarion call of freedom and liberated pleasure, has turned out to be a weak, vulnerable thing needing constant coddling by an army of agony aunts and sex therapists. And because it never quite delivers, people end up thumbing through a copy of *Fifty Shades of Grey*, or making yet more swipes of the Tinder app, or another visit to a pornography site. Or maybe a trip down to the gym . . .

Fulfilling relationships?

Let's look now at the quality of our relationships more generally. In his groundbreaking book *Bowling Alone* political scientist and Harvard professor Robert Putnam marshalled vast amounts of data to show how, compared with twenty-five years ago, Americans now belong to fewer organizations, sign fewer petitions, meet with friends less frequently, and socialize less often with their families.[7] They are living alone. And they are bowling alone too. More Americans than ever take part in the pastime of bowling, Putnam claims, but they are not bowling in leagues any more. They are 'bowling alone', hence the title of the book.

Several factors are in play here. As rates of living alone tend to be exacerbated during periods of recession, economic circumstances play a part. We also need to recognize the influence of changes in patterns of work, women's roles and population age-structure. But a significant part of this increase is related to a rise in numbers of people who divorce or break up after cohabitation. The rise among men particularly appears to be linked to the higher proportion that never marry at all. Also, when relationships break down, men are less likely to continue living with any children of the partnership.

We find a similar pattern in Great Britain where over the past few decades there has been a significant rise in the number of people living alone.[8] Again, we need to be careful in handling the data because trends vary by age group: for example, *fewer* young people are now living alone compared with a decade ago because more stay at home (unmarried) with parents. The bulk of the overall increase has been in the forty-five- to sixty-four-year-old age group where the number of people living alone has grown by 23 per cent in just a decade. Once again several factors (increased social mobility, welfare provision, urbanization) are in play, but a significant part of the increase is due to the number of people now divorced, single or who never marry at all.

But maybe living alone isn't such a bad thing? Maybe this is what flourishing looks like? Author and sociologist

Eric Klinenberg thinks so. In an interview about his book *Going Solo: The Extraordinary Rise and Surprising Appeal of Living Alone* he observes,

> Living alone in such large numbers is historically novel. I originally thought this change resulted from some social aberration. But then I discovered that living alone comports with our most sacred modern values: freedom, autonomy, control of one's time and space, and the search for individual fulfilment.[9]

Do you notice the 'sacred values' – freedom, autonomy, control of one's time and space, the search for individual fulfilment – that Klinenberg believes drive today's preference for solo living? They are the 'sacred values' of radical individualism: the cult of the individual.

And so, while only part of the rise in the proportion of people living alone is down to the breakdown of traditional marriage and family life, the core philosophy of the revolution, its radical individualism, continues to underpin it. This is the culture shift that plays into our modern preference for bowling alone.

Returning to our question, does it matter anyway? Klinenberg certainly thinks not. Among other benefits, he argues that being single delivers exhilarating new sexual freedoms. The idea that solo living is sexless and relationship-less is an anachronism, he says. There is a brave new world out there, and we need to get out there and grasp the nettle.

But does this argument stack up? I don't think so. A higher proportion of the population living alone is associated with higher levels of loneliness, especially for the elderly. More importantly, as Robert Putnam argues, living alone undermines community cohesion. And a healthy democracy depends on the active civic engagement of its citizens. Of course, for the young and fit, the surface attraction of pick-and-choose sexuality is easy to appreciate. There are endless possibilities, and when you have grown tired of one person, you can reconnect with another. The problems come downstream in a bowl-alone future of fragmented communities. Older people are put at risk of isolation and loneliness. Selfishness entrenches itself further in the human heart. And, as we shall see in the next chapter, impoverished communities are bad news for the most vulnerable of all – our children.

Of course, Christians should be among the first to underscore the pluses as well as the downsides to remaining unmarried (as does the apostle Paul). But in contrast to today's ethos of self-fulfilment, the Christian vision of solo living is about community and service – being part of something bigger than 'me'. It is orientated outwards in service and self-denial. In contrast, much contemporary solo living is rooted in the cult of the individual and pleasing yourself.

In the Christian vision, how we live now (whether single or married) carries big eternal consequences as well. What if 'bowling alone' is eternity's reward? In *The Great Divorce*, one of C. S. Lewis's most enthralling books, he takes his readers with him on a bus trip to heaven. But the story starts in hell, and it's a curious place. Lewis portrays hell as a vast town, with streets spreading far into the distance and over the horizon beyond. But the houses all around him stand empty, nobody at home:

'It seems the deuce of a town,' I volunteered, 'and that's what I can't understand. The parts that I saw were so empty. Was there once a much larger population?'

'Not at all,' said my neighbour. 'The trouble is that they're so quarrelsome. As soon as anyone arrives he settles in some street. Before he's been there twenty-four hours he quarrels with his neighbour. Before the week is over he's quarrelled so badly that he decides to move . . . finally he'll move right out to the edge of the town and build a new house. You see, it's easy here. You've only got to think a house and there it is. That's how the town keeps on growing.'

'Leaving more and more empty streets?'

'That's right . . . they've been moving on and on. Getting further apart.'[10]

Lewis's chilling picture of eternity is a place of fulfilled desire. You want to be alone? So be it. Bowling alone.

In this chapter we have explored the sexual revolution in terms of its failed promises of sexual fulfilment and flourishing relationships. But what about children? Where do they fit into its vision? The revolution's ambition for childhood appears to be a confused mixture of near-obsessive (and sadly necessary) requirements for more safeguarding and endless calls for more 'sex education' that nobody quite knows how to define. Sadly, the revolution has little positive vision for what a good childhood looks like and seems extraordinarily adult-orientated in its preoccupations. 'Adult shop' seems a well-chosen metaphor for the heartbeat of the revolution – shopping for adults. And yet, although children have little room in the revolution's ambitions, it is they who pay the biggest price of all for its failure. And so in the next chapter we will see how the retreat from marriage has helped heap inequalities and social injustice on the most vulnerable people of all – our children.

Key ideas in this chapter

- It is difficult to measure what is really going on in people's sex lives, so we need to treat media claims with caution and look carefully at what the data actually say.
- Surveys provide a consistent picture that rather than having more and better sex, the reverse is actually the case. Nobody knows why this is happening, but clearly the sexual revolution is failing to deliver on one of its central promises.
- Although more people are living alone, there is little evidence to suggest that they live happier, more fulfilling lives. Our modern preference for 'bowling alone' undermines community, civic society and wider human flourishing. And the consequences are eternal.

10 WAR ON THE WEAK

How kids pay the price of their parents' freedoms

.

After writing *Bowling Alone*, Robert Putnam continued to research the downstream effects of the collapse of American civil life and, in his most recent book *Our Kids: The American Dream in Crisis*, he tells us what he found.[1]

Putnam builds his case on the back of a raft of data and graphs, but there's passion here as well. The breakdown of community cohesion is heaping inequality on the most vulnerable members of society – our children. Putnam argues that it's time to start taking notice of what is happening to our kids, and he's right. As the sexual revolution continues to unfold, we need to focus upon its weakest victims, and turn towards our children.

Nineteen-million-more-word kids versus the rest

Putnam's thesis is that children's access to the key resources that foster personal development and well-being – cohesive communities, great schools and strong families – is becoming increasingly unequal and unfair, and that the situation is deteriorating fast. Meet one of Putnam's research subjects who sits at the bottom end of the privilege scale. He's a kid whose parents 'couldn't live together for nothing'. Subjected to a parade of feckless male role models and a revolving door of different carers, this boy gets through life as best he can, but basically he's home alone. At the other end of the scale, meet another of his subjects whose experience couldn't be more different. His parents fight to get him a place at the best school, turn up to cheer on the soccer pitch, and spend as long as it takes helping with his homework.

These two kids are so far apart in their experience of life they may as well be living on different planets. One difference stands out for me especially: by the time they start pre-school, children from professional families have heard an average of *19 million more words* than children from poor backgrounds. In contrast to the 19-million-more-word kids, those at the bottom of the ladder barely stand a chance. And in today's society the differences just keep on getting bigger.

Society was not always so polarized, says Putnam.

So who's to blame for these injustices? As a social scientist, Putnam spotlights social and economic changes, such as greater job instability in the US economy, declining real wages, the loss of social capital that follows declines in civil and community life. Drug culture takes its deathly dues as well. But there are other factors. Some critics, notably sociologist W. Bradford Wilcox, Director of the US National Marriage Project, believe that while Putnam's analysis is compelling in many respects, he fails to give sufficient weight to the retreat from marriage and the fragmentation of family structure that followed.[2] Either way, while there are many different factors in play – economic, social and educational – the blessing of a stable home life, built on the foundation of a secure and committed relationship between two parents, is one of them. Let's look into this a little further.

Marriage: the preserve of the rich

One of the paradoxes of modern life is that while the culture of marriage has collapsed in poorer communities, it seems to have stabilized, and may even be strengthening, among the better off. Take a look at the data for the UK, where the Office for National Statistics divides workers into seven social categories, with occupations such as company directors and university lecturers at the top end, and cleaners and waiters at the bottom end. According to one study, back in 2001 there was already a pretty big marriage gap when those in the top category were 24 per cent more likely to marry than those at the bottom. Since then that figure has doubled to 48 per cent.

The journalist who commissioned these data comments,

> So a marriage gap that barely existed a generation or
> two ago has managed to double in the last decade with
> a minimum of public debate. Somehow marriage, with all
> the advantages that it confers, is becoming the preserve
> of the rich.[3]

Even as they undermine its importance for everybody else, today's liberal elites seem to know something about marriage that they are keeping for themselves. But it is the poor and less educated who pay the price. The last great experiment with the ideological dismantling of the traditional family happened almost exactly 100 years ago after the Russian Revolution, and the outcome for the poorest was the same. One commentator writes,

Men took to changing wives with the same zest which
they displayed in the consumption of the recently restored
forty-per-cent vodka . . . Peasant boys looked upon marriage
as an exciting game and changed wives with the change of
seasons. It was not an unusual occurrence for a boy of
twenty to have had three or four wives, or for a girl of the
same age to have had three or four abortions.[4]

It took Joseph Stalin to reverse the policies that wreaked such
havoc among the poor.

In keeping with this overall pattern, the retreat from
marriage in the US hits African-American and poor communities the hardest of all. And the story continues to
unfold. In the States the collapse of marriage appears to be
creeping up the income ladder and spreading to the middle
class too. And with surprising speed, as W. Bradford Wilcox
observes:

Wherever we look among the communities that make
up the bedrock of the American middle class . . . the data
tell the same story: Divorce is high, non-marital childbearing
is spreading, and marital bliss is in increasingly short
supply.[5]

This spread to middle-income groups does not augur well for
the future either:

For if marriage is increasingly unachievable for our moderately
educated citizens – 58% of the adult population (age 25–60) –
then it is likely that we will witness the emergence of a new
society . . . children's life chances will diminish, and large
numbers of young men will live apart from the civilizing
power of married life.[6]

The magic of marriage?

These are bold claims. But can we be sure that marriage is the important ingredient here? Could it simply be the case that the kinds of people who get married tend to be those who possess the qualities that deliver better outcomes for kids? In other words, there is nothing magical about 'marriage' – it's the personal, economic and social conditions of those who are more likely to get married that counts.

If this line of argument is correct, then governments that want to help kids with poor life chances should target resources on reducing poverty and improving education, rather than being diverted into hopelessly ineffective campaigns to promote marriage.

So who is right? Does marriage have a magic ingredient all its own? Let's briefly work through what we know.

What good is marriage?

Before we go any further, let's get one thing clear. Successful families that deliver great outcomes for kids *come in all shapes and sizes*. There are many traditional-style marriages that harm and abuse the children in their care. And children blessed with love and diligent care can be found in all kinds of non-traditional arrangements. We need to celebrate good childcare wherever it is found.

But this should not deter us from having a vision of the ideal and of what works in the best interests of children overall. In other words, it is perfectly possible to acknowledge the numerous exceptions while still holding to the general rule. And looking at the evidence, the rule is clear: kids raised by two biological parents in a stable marriage do better, on average, than children raised in other family structures.

Take this conclusion from a review of ten years of family research, released recently in a joint report from Princeton University and the US Brookings Institution:

> Most scholars now agree that children raised by two biological parents in a stable marriage do better than children in other family forms across a wide range of outcomes.[7]

Another researcher puts it like this:

> Reams of social science and medical research convincingly show that children who are raised by their married, biological parents enjoy better physical, cognitive and emotional outcomes, on average, than children who are raised in other circumstances.[8]

We still haven't got to the heart of the matter though. While there isn't much debate about *whether* marriage is associated with better outcomes, there is less consensus about *why*. The confusion stems from the fact that you can't carry out carefully controlled experiments in this area: it isn't very easy to randomly allocate children to different kinds of family structures, and then compare outcomes a few years later! And so the question remains unresolved – is the compelling link between marriage and better life chances for kids just an association that can be explained by something else (such as the kind of people who get married), or does marriage have a magic of its own? This debate is awash with claim and counter-claim.

In the red corner stand those arguing that marriage only appears to work because it acts as a marker for good parenting and hard-working people. You could achieve the same outcomes by valuing hard work and raising standards of parenting – whatever family structure you choose to raise your kids in.

Over in the blue corner it is argued that, yes, marriage does predict better economic achievement and upward mobility, but that is because *the culture of commitment that comes with marriage* fosters virtues of hard work and parenting with high expectations. In other words, the commitment of marriage begins with love, but then builds a supporting cultural scaffold – promises sworn before a supportive community – for when love falters. Pointing to various statistical analyses, blue-corner advocates conclude that the data 'strongly suggest that marriage is more than the sum of these particular parts' and 'the advantages of marriage for children's wellbeing are likely to be hard to replicate through policy interventions other than those that bolster marriage itself'.[9]

OK, no surprises here, I am in the blue corner. I think marriage has a magic all its own. A society that values strong, committed marriages will, by default, nurture the virtues that are critical to the well-being of children: keeping promises, delayed gratification, commitment for the long haul, a focus on education, the blessings of self-control. We can call this the *stability factor*: it underpins a virtuous circle that puts education, work, marriage and childbearing in that order, one after the other. In a culture that values marriage these virtues become embedded in family life and recycled on to the next generation.

But then I would say that, wouldn't I? Yet this needn't be a zero-sum game. There are policy implications that can be implemented on both sides of this debate. There are key interventions for kids from poor backgrounds that need to be carried through by responsible government – the provision of better education, improved parenting resources, and benefit regimes that reward responsible care. Christians should be at the forefront of lobbying in the fight for social justice.

On the other side of the debate governments should also do what they can to promote marriage by adopting intelligent policies (such as smarter tax policies that incentivize stable relationships). But the promotion of marriage is a particular calling for churches. As Putnam says, governments are not particularly good at promoting marriage. Churches need to rise to this challenge. The promotion of strong marriages and families is potentially one of our most fruitful contributions to the common good.

Divorce and cohabitation: children pay the price

Let's look further into the impact of divorce and cohabitation on kids. In the 1970s, as the sexual revolution got under way, divorce rates rocketed in the UK. The number of divorces then levelled, and since 1985 the raw numbers have remained relatively stable, even falling slightly.[10] So what's the problem? The problem is cohabitation. In the UK cohabiting couple families grew by 29.7 per cent between 2004 and 2014, and this is now the fastest-growing type of family structure in the UK.[11]

This trend spells bad news for kids. Once again we need to underscore that this is a general rule with countless exceptions. Sometimes, for example, a parental separation is simply the best option for kids. But the exceptions mustn't blind us to the rule: the case for staying together for the sake of the children is much stronger than many suppose.[12]

Cohabiting couples can be great parents. Of course they can. But cohabitation is much less stable than marriage. In a study from the UK Marriage Foundation the author found that, independent of mothers' age or education, more than half of couples who only get married after the birth of their first child have split up ten years later, compared with only one-quarter of couples who marry *before* having children. And where cohabiting couples with children do not marry at all, a whopping *two-thirds* have split up. The same source calculates that the trend away from marriage since 1980 may have cost up to 1.8 million children the chance to grow up with both parents.[13]

And so divorce isn't the biggest threat for kids today; it's the seemingly unstoppable rise of cohabitation. As a result of these social trends, 48 per cent of all children born today will not be found living with both natural parents by their sixteenth birthday, a substantial increase over the 40 per cent figure estimated ten years previously.[14] And here is the important news – failing marriages ending in divorce account for only 20 per cent of break-ups. The break-up of cohabiting families accounts for the other 80 per cent.

We are talking about 1.8 million individual lives here, impacted during their most formative and foundational years. And the general principle is clear – insecurity and instability are bad for kids in terms of almost any outcome that you care to mention. Thankfully, kids are remarkably resilient, and most do not suffer the more serious emotional and personal consequences. But many do, and the effects are well documented. For example, analysis using the Millennial Cohort Study carried out in the UK examined longer-term mental health outcomes among 10,448 eleven-year-olds. Overall, 18.1 per cent of those living in stepfamilies had significant mental health problems, compared to 15 per cent of those living with single parents and 6.6 per cent of those living with both natural parents. Boys were affected most of all, displaying conduct problems, hyperactivity and attention-deficit issues.

The sad reality for these children is that while fathers who stay in the family home tend to be more engaged today in their children's lives, those who split from the family home (and it is usually the fathers who leave) are much less likely to be involved in the lives of the children they leave behind. Twenty-seven per cent pay no visits at all and another 21 per cent only see their kids 'several times a year'. Thirty-one per cent call or email their kids 'less than once a month', and another 28 per cent only contact them between one and four times a month.[15] Don't let the raw data lull you into complacency – this is simply an outrage.

We are in danger of information overload, but these data underscore what the magic of marriage really is. Marriage creates a culture that binds men to their responsibilities for the children they bring into the world. It cements social expectations that boys and men will develop the virtues of commitment and faithfulness necessary to build strong marriages – for the well-being of kids and the life of our communities as a whole.

The irony, as we noted earlier, is that these huge cultural shifts have taken their toll on lower-income families, while among the educational elites that imposed their progressive views on the rest of society the marriage trend appears to be heading in the opposite direction. After imposing their liberal views on the poorest, the better off are reaping the benefits of marriage for themselves. These are issues of inclusion and justice. The goods and benefits of marriage are for all – not least a generation of poorer kids now bearing the brunt of our failures.

'Basically . . . porn is everywhere'

Then there's the long shadow that pornography casts over childhood. The Office of the Children's Commissioner (a body established by the UK Government to promote the rights and interests of children in policies or decisions affecting their lives) recently commissioned a report into the effects of pornography on young people. Its title: '"Basically . . . porn is everywhere"' pretty much sums up its main conclusion.[16]

The report cautiously acknowledges that much of the research is of poor quality, and it is difficult to unravel what causes what. There is solid evidence of a link between exposure to pornography and 'risky behaviours' such as unprotected oral or anal sex, for example, but the evidence simply isn't good enough to allow conclusions about causation. It is equally difficult to figure out whether exposure to violent pornography actually causes violent sexual behaviours, or whether the same types of people tend to engage in both. So there is still a lot of work to be done. What is clear, however, is the huge proportion of children and young people now exposed to, or who access, pornography.

The pornographication of childhood

The result is that the majority of children, especially boys, receive their sex education today courtesy of the pornography industry. Studies conducted in different countries report a range of 43 per cent to 99 per cent for childhood exposure to pornography, with rates for boys rising to between 83 per cent and 100 per cent.[17] Data for the age of *first* exposure are more contradictory, with some reporting significant numbers at age ten or eleven years, while others offer slightly higher average ages. It is important to note, however, that young people are not simply viewing images – *they are being educated by them*. Besides porn's explicit messages about the essentially hedonistic and self-serving meaning of sex, minds are being formed around the treatment of people as sex objects and the creeping normalization of sadomasochistic and other extreme behaviours.

So can we lay the pornographication of childhood at the door of the sexual revolution too? We need to avoid drawing simplistic conclusions. Porn has been around for centuries, and arguably its ready availability on children's smart-phones and laptops is a product of the technological, rather than the sexual, revolution. And few people with otherwise liberal attitudes to sexuality would support these levels of exposure to porn among the young.

My point, however, is that while the sexual revolution may not be directly responsible for the spread of porn, its ideology offers little that is capable of resisting it. The report from the Children's Commissioner laudably highlights the way that pornography affects children's beliefs about promiscuity and casual sex, but ducks the hard questions: what is the moral case against casual sex, provided it is done 'safely', and why? These are ethical judgments that sit within people's moral frameworks. In today's climate of freedom and 'choice', on what basis do we instruct teenagers about the rights and wrongs of what they do with their bodies?

Reports of pornography use among children, and the current epidemic of 'sexting' are accompanied ritualistically by calls for 'more sex education'. The sad reality, however, is that most sex education, when it happens at all, is too little, too late, and confined to the mechanics, rather than the meaning, of sex. And that is the central challenge to the revolution. Beyond the usual calls for freedom and acceptance, what is the sexual revolution's vision of *what sex is for*?

Our children need a richer moral framework than one built on vague generalizations of inclusion and diversity. At some point we must grasp the nettle: whose morals? Which worldview? I am not arguing here that moral frameworks cannot be generated by alternatives to the Christian worldview, but simply that we cannot escape the challenge of worldview. Vague notions of freedom and 'just being yourself' marketed by today's media-driven individualism simply won't do. It is a house of cards. And as we shall see further in the next chapter on fragmenting identities, it is our children who continue to pay the price.

Key ideas in this chapter

- Access to the key resources that foster the development and well-being of children – cohesive communities, great schools and strong families – is unequal and unfair, and the situation is deteriorating fast.
- While several factors are responsible for this injustice, the retreat from marriage over recent decades has played a critical role. A stable home life, built on a committed relationship of two biological parents, is associated with a range of better life chances for kids.
- Divorce isn't the biggest threat for kids today, but rather the seemingly unstoppable rise of cohabitation. Cohabiting relationships are much less stable, and instability damages the social and emotional health of children.
- While it is impossible to prove conclusively, there is evidence that marriage has a 'magic' of its own in helping to build stronger families. Marriage creates a culture that binds men to their responsibilities for the children they help to bring into the world; it fosters expectations that boys and men will develop virtues of commitment and faithfulness.
- The pornographication of childhood is almost symbolic of the revolution's inability to provide a moral framework robust enough for true human flourishing. The revolution has a clear idea of what it is against, but

what is it for? Beyond vague notions of inclusion and diversity, the revolution seems to have little that is positive to say about the true nature and meaning of sex and sexuality.

11 WHO AM I TODAY?

The treadmill of self-identification

'Just be your real self!' This is more than a suggestion – it's a promise. The modern clarion call to authenticity, being true to the self within, markets the prospect of a stronger, more durable sense of core identity. It's about freedom and flourishing, and, as a result, we are more obsessed than ever with questions of identity. But has the revolution delivered on its promises? In today's world of self-expression is it getting any easier to be 'me'?

There is no simple agreed definition of identity, but for our purposes I take identity to refer to the inner 'core' that allows people to move between different social roles while retaining a sense of being one and the same person.[1] It is the story we tell ourselves about ourselves: the inner narrative that gives a sense of meaning and coherence to our lives.

The challenge to coherence

The pace and scale of the cultural and technological changes of the past few decades make it increasingly difficult to achieve this sense of stability and coherence. In the past people settled into relatively stable patterns quite early on in their life cycle – a long-term job, getting married, bearing children. Now the transition from adolescence to adulthood stretches into the early thirties, with an ever-widening range of possibilities offering vastly increased options for how to be 'me' today.

Even more significant is the rise of hyper-connectivity, which is about being constantly connected to social networks and streams of information. It is estimated that in 2011 there were more devices connected to the Internet than the number of people in the world, and numbers go on rising.[2] It is difficult to predict fully the impact of these changes, but as people experience technologically mediated blurring of the boundaries between social life, work and home, it becomes ever more difficult to maintain a distinctive sense of being a separate self.

Further, social media offers new platforms for the development of online identities. With apps available for smoothing out wrinkles or applying artificial make-up, you can now present (and re-present) yourself to the world in highly editable formats. The more radical option of cosmetic surgery has also boomed in Western culture over the past few years. In a recent poll by the American Academy of Facial Plastic and Reconstructive Surgery 64 per cent of plastic surgeons reported an increase in the use of cosmetic surgery or injectable treatments in patients under thirty, which was mostly attributed to the influence of social media images.[3]

The possibility of creating a virtual online identity is another radical new departure. Some individuals feel they only achieve their 'true' identity when in role as their avatar:

> I have a lot of physical disabilities in real life, but in Star Wars Galaxies I can ride an imperial speeder bike, fight monsters or just hang out with friends at the bar.[4]

In response to these developments we might argue that people have faced social upheavals of one kind or another throughout history, so has anything really changed? I think that there is in fact something new and potentially sinister about our technology-driven contemporary culture. What makes the present moment so unique is the convergence of fast-moving changes that blur the boundaries of reality with a radical individualism that redefines it. Indeed, as we saw in chapter 2, this whole area brings into focus, in a big way, the question: 'What is real?'

But why should we care?

On the face of it the modern project of self-construction offers exhilarating new freedoms. Contemporary culture places before us a smorgasbord of possibilities for self-invention, and when we grow tired of one option, we may simply choose another. And why not?

The problem is obvious. In a world of limitless choice and endless possibility, with no guide or map to provide us with an external point of reference, how do we choose between competing realities? As we look within, which facet of experience will help us decide today? Should we follow this fleeting thought or that whim? Should it be this feeling or that impulse?

Or perhaps it's all about getting in touch with one's inner hero. But what if your inner hero turns out to be elusive? What if the self you discover within turns out to be a weak, vulnerable and rather dependent thing? And what if your suspicion grows that the notion of your inner hero itself has simply been marketed to you? And you swallowed it hook, line and sinker? In a manipulative consumerist culture, far from being the architects of our own destiny, maybe the whole idea of inventing ourselves is just another thing we've been sold, and the real driver isn't the individual at all.

Compare these two situations. A couple of centuries ago an educated young woman approaching her twenty-first birthday 'looks within' and discovers a strong desire to be married, to run a household and to have children. All well and good. But she also discovers another impulse at work alongside the first: she wants to run something bigger than a household: a farm maybe, or perhaps even become a politician. She knows she could do it. But the social conventions of her time will lead her to suppress the latter set of desires and nurture the former.

Fast forward to the same young woman today just completing the second of a three-year university degree. Only now the thing she most wants is to marry and have lots of children with the love of her life. Today even to think about settling down with a family so early would be deemed irresponsible. And to waste her talents and narrow her life choices in this way would, frankly, seem almost immoral given the vast amounts of money her parents have invested in her education. Her culture shouts, 'Be yourself!' but then sets a very clear boundary around what that is permitted to look like.

Regardless of the rights and wrongs of these two different situations, my point is simply that this capable woman is less free than she thinks. You may counter that at least today she has a much wider range of options. That is true. But it would be foolish to ignore the force of today's cultural expectations about how she should choose. The power of culture to shape attitudes and expectations is no less today; it is simply better at deceiving us into thinking we have more freedom.

So, having reviewed the contradictions at the heart of the modern quest for self-identification, and the cultural changes causing increasing fragmentation, let's turn to consider some of the consequences.

The consequences of self-identification

Risks to mental health and well-being

First, there are risks to mental health. The possession of a relatively stable sense of self is integral to healthy psychological development and well-being. Without a stable inner core to give coherence and purpose, we find it harder to resist short-term rewards and stick to longer-term objectives. We are more at the mercy of other people's expectations, tossed about on the shifting currents of culture and environment. We feel empty and alone. As a result, it is plausible (although not at the moment provable) that a recent increase in self-harm among young people is at least partly attributable to this modern fragility of the self.[5]

The ability to act effectively and confidently, to give love and receive it, also requires a sense of self-worth and significance. But if the self is constantly in flux, a shifting sand of doubt and reinvention, how can such a delicate thing sustain a sense of its own worth and value? The deceit of the self-esteem movement has been to suggest that worth and value can simply be asserted: 'I'm special!' 'I attract people to me now!' 'Think positively!' But as studies have shown, rather than producing new improved versions of the self, these attempts at self-affirmation leave people with low self-worth feeling more depressed than ever.[6]

The modern self is simply too weak, too insecure, to sustain a sense of its own worth. Self-affirmation, like self-identification, backfires for the people who need it most. In fact, there's good evidence that the pursuit of self-esteem for its own sake drives people back into yet more striving and yet more approval seeking.[7] It's hard to believe your own propaganda, and that's all it is after all.

Risks to society and relationships

Second, issues of identity are important for the quality of our relationships and the ability to form cooperative communities. Good relationships depend upon a capacity to anticipate the needs of other people, and to respond to them in predictable ways. This is especially important in families where stability is fundamental to the healthy development of children. But when individuals are changing aspects of their personality, or more dramatically, their sex, age or ethnicity, stability is undermined. And because a fragmented, weak identity constantly puts your self-worth at stake, empathy is reduced as well. Few emotional resources are available for others when so much care and attention needs to be expended upon yourself.

Victimhood identity and the chilling of free speech

Third, the fragility of identity appears to be connected with a growing obsession with the self-protection observed on many university campuses. For some, often among the most vocal and politically engaged, identity seems to be founded upon a kind of victimhood status. Visiting speakers whose views may offend are being 'de-platformed' or their lectures hedged with 'trigger warnings' in order to protect the vulnerable and unsuspecting from offence or psychological harm.

This pursuit of 'safe spaces' on campuses projects the self as inherently fragile and wounded, in need of cosseting and protection. Of course, every society must consider what limits to impose on the propagation of potentially harmful ideas, but victimhood identity consolidates the notion of the self as weak and constantly at risk. It poses a self so vulnerable, in fact, that reality itself must be made to conform to its needs.

Risks to developing gender identity

Finally, identity confusion is encountered most frequently today in the sphere of gender. As we noted in chapter 2, this is a complicated area in which a little information can be dangerous. If you want to know more, psychologist Mark Yarhouse has drawn together a scholarly review of the academic material in his book, *Understanding Gender Dysphoria*.[8]

We need to reconsider this phenomenon briefly, however, because, as we noted earlier, the experience of a small minority of people is being used to justify a new gender ideology being imposed upon the majority. This not only affects what pronoun you might use to address a person with gender dysphoria out of respect for their inner sense of conflict, but it calls into question whether we should use pronouns based upon a person's biological sex at all. As a result, we are witnessing calls for the removal of sex as an identifying characteristic on passports and other personal documents. Even more concerning is the pace at which children are being drawn into this new paradigm. Children are being told that gender is 'fluid' and that the biggest clue to gender is not found in the shape of your body but in the state of your mind.

The problem here is that attempts to meet the needs of the few (no matter how well intentioned) risk confusion and harm for the many. Children and young people are being subject to an untried and untested social experiment involving potential interference with their gender identity development that has until now proceeded perfectly satisfactorily for the vast majority. Further, as we noted earlier, the logic of self-identification is being applied well beyond questions of gender (for example, to age, ethnicity and species), and nobody knows what the end game will be. We have simply no idea how these new ways of thinking about being human will play out, and of the risks they pose to human flourishing and the well-being of children. Even some secularists, who would normally part company with traditional Christian moral values, are beginning to have serious doubts about the latest twists in this ongoing revolution.

Concluding thoughts

In the last few chapters the promises of the sexual revolution have been weighed in the balance and found wanting. We have been careful to acknowledge that it isn't all bad news, however: the revolution has ushered in important new freedoms and opportunities, especially for women. Those previously pushed to the margins have found justice and social inclusion, and we should welcome and celebrate these developments. But when we stand back and survey the entire landscape of the revolution, we witness injustice heaped upon children, more people than ever living alone, the collapse of marriage among the poor, fatherless wastelands of social deprivation, and the pornographication of childhood.

One of the core messages of the gospel is that idols always ask for more and more, but give less and less, until in the end they have everything and you have nothing. And so it is here. The irony is that after the revolution, even as they continue to obsess over their identities, people are not even having more or better sex than before. The core ideas of the revolution – 'be yourself', 'find the you within' – appear to be just another idolatry.

This isn't a moment for gloating, but for lamentation. Orthodox Christians, with their sub-biblical shame culture, paved the way for much of the sexual revolution. And as the revolution got under way, our cowardly inability to articulate an alternative vision of sexual flourishing remains a continuing source of shame: it is we who have been weighed in the balance and found wanting. We will not develop a genuinely radical response to the revolution until we have fully owned the responsibility we share. And we shall never speak with conviction about good news for the world until that battle is won in our own hearts.

So in part 3 we turn finally to ask: we need a better story, but what does it look like? How should we respond? And where do we start? As we have seen in this chapter, after five decades of unravelling, the sexual revolution is now posing the biggest question of all: what does it mean to be human? And that is where our own story needs to begin.

Key ideas in this chapter

- Identity refers to a sense of having an inner core that allows us to move between different roles while retaining a sense of being the same person. It is the inner story that gives meaning and coherence to our lives.
- Major cultural and technological changes mean that it is increasingly difficult to form and sustain this inner coherence, and radical individualism is making it harder than ever. What makes the present moment so unique, however, is the convergence of fast-moving changes that blur the boundaries of reality with a radical individualism that attempts to redefine it.
- The resulting confusion heightens risks to mental health and social cohesion. It underpins victimhood identities and growing confusion about our bodies and gender fluidity. These risks may be especially dangerous for young people and children in the most formative years of their lives.

Part 3

A BETTER STORY

12 LIVING IN GOD'S REALITY

Our story begins when we are welcomed into God's reality

You can't respond to a great story with a list of facts. Well, you can, of course, but hardly anybody will listen. If you want to win hearts as well as minds, you need to tell a better story. But where do we begin?

A narrative, remember, puts facts and ideas together in ways which the mind finds interesting and memorable. So that's where we'll begin, by gathering together the relevant facts and ideas that will eventually fashion the plot lines of our story.

Earlier in this book we explored the core ideas and facts about the revolution in the shape of modern Gnosticism and radical individualism. What are the key insights about sex and relationships that sit at the heart of the Christian narrative? What do *we* think sex between human beings is about? And the biggest question of all: what is it *for*?

I am going to begin with the five core convictions that will shape the way we try to answer these questions. Together these 'big five' are the foundational pillars on which everything else in our story eventually comes to rest.

Five pillars of the Christian vision for sex and marriage

God has spoken: you don't have to figure it all out for yourself
First, the biblical understanding of sex is, well, *biblical*. God has revealed it to human beings, and it is centred in his character and purpose. The secular narrative resonates with subplots that revolve around 'me' rather than God. These plots tell how I seized power, commandeered the script and started to write the story myself. Today's radical individualism is remarkably consistent with its own starting point. If your worldview is premised on the conviction that you stand alone in a meaningless universe, the modern project of self-identification has a painful logic: life is what you make of it, and so is reality itself. You become the principal actor in life's drama because you have no other choice.

The gospel repudiates this foregrounding of the self. Its vision of the purpose and meaning of sex is grounded in the big truth that God has revealed himself and that we don't have to figure it all out for ourselves. God has spoken in his Son Jesus Christ and his written Word, the Bible. This simple but fundamental truth is the most important of the five pillars on which the whole biblical vision for human sexuality is founded.

God welcomes you into a reality of his making, not yours
Second, God welcomes human beings into *his* reality. We humans don't stand above or separate from God's reality – we are part of it. In other words, we are *creatures*. This simple fact has far-reaching implications for our basic psychological posture towards the world and our place in it. It means that whatever we see as our calling and purpose in this world, it needs to be with a sense of humble submission to its Creator and our creaturely dependence on him. The gospel calls

us to learn to be God's creature all over again. This is his reality, not ours.

We flourish as human beings when we work with, rather than against, the grain of God's reality

The third foundational truth says that we flourish as human beings when we work in harmony with God's reality. Human beings are a very special kind of creature: pivotal creatures fashioned in the image of God and called to have dominion over all that he declared good (Genesis 1:26–28). The creation narratives tell us that the world was created with a natural sense of 'fit' between these new creatures in God's image and the world into which they had been placed.[1] The world was created with these god-like creatures in mind, and they will flourish as they work with the grain of God's reality, and not against it.

What do I mean by the *grain* of reality? I mean that reality has been created with a certain 'way' built into it, an ingrained pattern that points towards a particular goal or truth. Look at the opening verses of Psalm 19:

> The heavens declare the glory of God;
> the skies proclaim the work of his hands.
> Day after day they pour forth speech;
> night after night they reveal knowledge.
> (Psalm 19:1–2)

Do you see what this means? Despite the disfiguring effects of the fall, reality is still one of our greatest teachers. And its first and greatest lesson is to teach us about our Creator. Thus nature not only proclaims the glory of God, but by 'revealing knowledge' to human beings, it helps them fulfil their purpose and calling to proclaim God's glory as well. And so, when a fully alive human being sits under a starry sky on a cloudless night, she finds herself giving thanks and glory to God because it is the *natural* thing to do. It is as though reality has a natural rhythm that invites us to tap our feet to its paean of praise.

Further, think about how Jesus appealed to nature's role in human instruction: 'Look at the birds of the air; they do not sow or reap or store away in barns, and yet your heavenly Father feeds them. Are you not much more valuable than they?' (Matthew 6:26). His practical advice not to be anxious appeals to our ability to look around God's reality and see how he cares for the rest of his creation.

The apostle Paul went further still. While preaching to the Athenian philosophers, he said, '[God] is not far from any one of us. "For in him we live and move and have our being." As some of your own poets have said, "We are his offspring"' (Acts 17:27–28). When Paul quoted their poets in this way, he was saying that even pagans could discern facets of God's character by listening to God speaking in the world around them.

The book of nature helps us to know how we can flourish as human beings too. We see this most clearly in Paul's letter to the Romans where he talks about God's judgment of Gentiles who 'suppress the truth' (Romans 1:18). God's anger against idol worshippers is justified, Paul says, because they should know better: the majesty and beauty of God is writ large across creation for all to see. But then he goes on to say that reality also has lessons to teach us about God's moral law – even Gentiles 'do by nature things required by the law' since the law has been 'written on their hearts' (Romans 2:14–15). In other words, norms of morality and human flourishing have been etched into the order of creation for all to see.

The bottom line of all this is that in creation God welcomes humankind into a reality that both speaks of his glory *and* points them to ways of life that please him. When we adopt the psychological posture of a creature, and work in harmony with God's reality, we are on the road to becoming fully human. And so the road to human flourishing, and to God's glory, is to work *with* the grain of God's reality, not to try to manufacture a reality of our own.

But what about the effect of human sin? You may argue that, yes, creation proclaims God's glory, but it also portrays – only too clearly – the ugliness and degradation brought about by human sin. Further, as Paul taught, because sinful human minds are disposed to suppress and distort the truth, they discern the things of God '[as] through a glass, darkly' (1 Corinthians 13:12, KJV). How can we work with the grain of a reality that is so broken and hard to see?

The answer is that we can't rely on general revelation in the book of nature alone. We need the big picture. We need the revelation of Scripture. Ultimately, therefore, along with everything else, our understanding of the biblical vision for sex and relationships is rooted in what we know because of the gospel. Nature still sings, albeit sometimes with faltering voice, to the glory of God. God's ways can still be seen, even in shadowy form, in our fallen world. There are still strong signals in nature about the natural ways of being human. But the resurrection of Jesus is the first-fruits of a reality that will one day be fully restored. Let's call it a *greater reality*. This greater reality has already burst in, in the resurrected body of the living Christ, and it is this hope that now welcomes us. And so true human flourishing is found in working towards this greater reality, even though, at the moment, it is discerned only faintly in this fallen world.

God not only reveals who he is, but he reveals who we are as well
Fourth, human identity is not discovered within the self, nor
autonomously constructed by the self; it is revealed to the self.
God speaks our identity to us. In other words, God not only
reveals who he is; he shows us who we are. Jesus calls his sheep
'by name' (John 10:3), and those who receive him are given
authority to be called 'children of God' (John 1:12; 1 John 3:2).
They are divine image-bearers, each being restored in Christ,
each known individually and named by God.

And so, because God has spoken to us in this way, Christians
repudiate the entire infrastructure of self-construction as too
emaciated and deficient to bear the weight of being human.
Characteristics such as gender, race, nationality and sexuality
are important, but we reject the modern practice of elevating
these part identities into whole identities. Nothing less than
the whole glory of the restored image of God in humankind
will do. That is our identity. That is who we are.

But what does this look like? 'My identity is in Christ' rolls
off the tongue, but a simple statement of the facts like this is
also too weak to resist the counter-narratives of our culture.
We need to inhabit our identity *imaginatively*. What does this
mean? Think of your identity in Christ as a two-sided coin.
On one side we find our creaturely identity, in the sense that
we are made in the 'image' and 'likeness' of God (Genesis
1:26–27). Because we are like God, therefore, our creaturely
way of being in the world, so to speak, needs to echo the ways
of God himself. We are called to love as he loves, to rule as
he rules. So next time you switch on the vacuum cleaner,
chair a committee meeting, pick up the kids from school,
mend a tyre, diagnose a heart condition, remember – *imagine*
– the greater reality that you are imaging in your work. You
are bringing order to the world as he brought order. You are
taking part in the restoration of all things in Christ. Bear his

image with dignity and pride. Like him, try to rule with compassion and justice, and with a heart for the poor. Practise living consistently with your creaturely identity in Christ, asking the Holy Spirit to help you fulfil the true nature of your calling.

Now look on the other side of the coin. Here we discover our *redemptive identity*. Although God's image in us has been disfigured by the fall, it is being restored after the image of his Son, Jesus. And so becoming like Jesus transfigures our creaturely identity with even greater meaning and substance. We bear the image of Christ himself and, through the indwelling Spirit, we are already beginning to experience the first-fruits of transformation of character and temperament. John put it like this: 'Dear friends, now we are children of God, and what we will be has not yet been made known. But we know that when Christ appears, we shall be like him, for we shall see him as he is' (1 John 3:2).

These two dimensions of the self offer a thick view of human identity that isn't built on the shifting sands of self-identification and self-construction. It is a given identity, charged with purpose and meaning because it takes part in a story bigger than itself – the redemption of all things in Christ. To live out our identity, to work with the grain of our calling, is the basis of true freedom – our *natural* freedom – because at last we have found our unique place in the tapestry of God's redemptive story.

The task now facing the church is to reframe and embody these truths in ways that speak into modern culture, and inspire the hearts and imaginations of its own people as well.

No matter what happens, God is good

The fifth and final pillar states that no matter what happens, because of the cross of Christ, we know that God is good.

Because sin has distorted and broken the natural order of God's creation, his goodness can sometimes be hard to see. You may be thinking that it is easy to speak of inhabiting our 'identity in Christ', but it's slow painful work when your experience of child abuse has knitted shame into every fibre of your being. It can also be hard to discern the goodness in God's moral laws, especially when we focus on individual pain and suffering while forgetting the larger principles that may be at stake. So, for example, when confronted with dreadful pain and suffering, we ask how a good God could pile on the agony by denying the right to assisted suicide. Or we find ourselves asking how it can possibly be wrong to support a same-sex sexual relationship that seems so happy and life-giving.

These are valid and potent objections. We can point in response to the destruction wreaked on God's creation by human disobedience and pride; we can point out that we see only part of the picture whereas God sees the whole. These are valid and good arguments. But in the end there is a mystery in suffering: our creaturely minds are finite, and there are some things that only God knows and sees. But the Christian gospel is focused on the cross of Christ: God himself entered into the furthest reaches of human suffering and bled in our place. This doesn't answer all our questions, but it establishes the basis of our trust: we know that God is good because we see it revealed in the life and death of his Son, Jesus.

God has spoken, and we are not alone; he welcomes us into his reality, not one of our own making; we flourish when we work with the grain of his greater reality; God not only reveals who he is, he reveals who we are too; and no matter what happens, standing at the foot of the cross, we know that God is good. These are the five pillars on which the gospel understanding of sex and marriage rests.

Let's be honest, these seem so at odds with today's culture that you may feel like giving up right now. But don't be pessimistic. As the Roman poet Horace once pronounced, 'You may drive out Nature with a pitchfork, yet she still will hurry back.'[2] Even though badly disfigured by sin, we are still made in the image of God. And despite our terrifying capacity for wickedness and destruction, reality has a habit of eventually making itself known. As the revolution continues to unravel, our culture may be ready to hear the good news again sooner than we imagine.

So in this confidence, and building upon these five foundations, in the next chapter we will consider the biggest question of all: what is sex for? In the biblical vision, what do we see?

Key ideas in this chapter

- A good narrative puts information and ideas together in ways the mind finds interesting and memorable. So telling a better story about sex and relationships needs to start by gathering together the relevant biblical truths and ideas.
- The biblical understanding of sex and relationships is built upon five foundational pillars: God has spoken and we don't need to figure it out for ourselves. His Word, revealed in the book of nature, and more fully in the revelation of Scripture, welcomes us into his reality, and we flourish as we live with the grain of his reality. For the Christian, identity is not discovered within or self-constructed, but revealed by God and lived out in his reality. And finally, whatever happens, God is good. Building our vision on these foundations puts us on the road to flourishing.

- In the gospel God restores our identity to us as image-bearing children being conformed to the image of Christ. The more we live in harmony with this calling, working with the grain of God's reality rather than against it, the more we begin to flourish as followers of Christ.
- The road to flourishing is the way of the cross. Submitting to God – learning to be his creature – is hard, especially in today's culture of entitlement. But at the cross we see that God is good; we can trust him even when goodness is hard to see. And, enduring to the end, we shall see the face of God.

13 THE END OF LONGING

How our sexual desires connect us with heaven

In August 2001 an American TV channel aired an interview with Muhammad Abu Wardeh, a Hamas activist who had recruited a terrorist for suicide bombings in Israel. He was quoted as saying, 'I described to him how God would compensate the martyr for sacrificing his life for his land. If you become a martyr, God will give you 70 virgins, 70 wives and everlasting happiness.'[1]

There's a great deal of controversy about what the Qur'an really says about the link between acts like suicide bombing and their sexual rewards. But there was no confusion in this activist's mind, despite the fact that he was actually short-changing his potential recruits: the reward is usually quoted as the opportunity for unlimited sex with seventy-two virgins.

What is less controversial, however, is Islam's picture of heaven as a garden paradise that includes sexual delight. Wardeh defrauded his recruits on this count too, because dark-eyed virgins are said to be available to all Muslims, not just martyrs. Liberal scholars of Islam emphasize the metaphorical nature of these rumoured goings-on in paradise, but there is no denying the sensuous and graphic descriptions offered by some traditional Qur'anic commentators. Al-Suyuti, who lived in the fourteenth century, wrote that 'each time we sleep with a *houri* [sexual partner in paradise] we find her a virgin. Besides, the penis of the Elected never softens. The erection is eternal.'[2]

On the face of it the breathless delights of paradise in Islamic tradition stand in stark contrast to the Christian version of heaven. Jesus summed up the Christian picture brusquely: 'At the resurrection people will neither marry nor be given in marriage; they will be like the angels in heaven' (Matthew 22:30). And that's it. C. S. Lewis captured the problem in typical style:

> The letter and spirit of Scripture, and of all Christianity, forbid us to suppose that life in the new creation will be a sexual life [in the sense of people having sex together] . . . this reduces our imagination to the withering alternatives either of bodies which are hardly recognisable as human bodies or else of a perpetual fast.[3]

This is not a particularly appetizing prospect.

So what is the Christian vision of sex? How do our deepest desires, including our most earthy, bodily longings for intimacy, connect with the promise of heaven?

Sex is both a taster and a picture of divine love

'There will be no marriage in heaven,' says Jesus. Actually that isn't what he says. Jesus says, 'At the resurrection *people* will neither marry nor be given in marriage . . .' The Bible does not teach that there will be no marriage in heaven. Rather, it teaches there will be *one* marriage in heaven – between Christ and his bride, the church.

So how do we square this circle? On the one hand, there will be no actual sexual relationships between people in the new order because in this respect they will have angel-like qualities. On the other hand, the union between God and his people is described as a marriage. Why deploy the marriage metaphor at all (as opposed, say, to the more straightforward language of contract) unless it is being used to describe a union of a *particular kind*?

In fact, the biblical picture of marital sexual union is nothing less than an *anticipation* of an even deeper union with the Divine. And whether we are married or single in this life, sexual desire is our inbuilt homing instinct for the Divine, a kind of navigation aid showing us the way home. You could think of it as a form of body language: our bodies talk to us about a greater reality of fulfilment and eternal blessing, and urge us to go there.

Born to love

It turns out that our bodies begin to talk in this way from the moment of our birth. Within the first twenty-four hours newborns are already beginning to explore the wonders of their environment. Of course, it takes time for their eyes to learn to work together and move between images. And yet in the first few days of life, before these skills have been fully acquired, studies show that their eyes tend to track towards faces rather than geometric patterns. In other words, the newborn brain is primed with an inbuilt sensitivity for, and attraction to, face-like images. We enter the world with many interactions already primed to go – and relationships are at the top of the pack.

Soon the newborn's preferences for faces settles on one face in particular, namely that of the mother or principal caregiver.

It isn't hard to figure out why. Human beings are among the most developmentally immature of all the primates, requiring years of parental care to help them grow normally and reach their developmental potential. So it isn't surprising that infants are primed for that oh-so-seductive meeting of the eyes that will hook the attention of the persons whose care they need most. There's something almost *romantic* about it.

Mothers are biologically primed to reciprocate this romantic meeting of the eyes as well: the hormone oxytocin (mentioned in a previous chapter) takes care of that. Oxytocin, secreted through pregnancy and lactation, plays a crucial role in the tightening of the emotional bond between mother and baby. And as we know, the quality and stability (we could say *faithfulness*) of this bond turns out to be a crucial factor in long-term well-being: women who experienced poor-quality care in their own infancy find it harder to provide stable care themselves, and there are links to relationship problems, depression and anxiety too.[4]

Now, as we saw previously, there's been a lot of hype around oxytocin (the 'cuddle chemical'!) and we should avoid over-egging the evidence. Nevertheless, oxytocin does appear to play a crucial role in kindling, and then cementing, the life-enhancing bond between mother and baby that's so necessary for their flourishing. Oxytocin also appears to be involved in bonding between human beings more generally. Indeed, the eye-tracking pattern observed in the newborn is simply the first glimpse of how humans are primed for bonded relationships. Oxytocin then continues to facilitate these pro-social emotions of trust and affection throughout our lives.

Once these bonds have been formed – whether in monogamous pair bonding, parent–child bonding or wider friendship bonding – there is a price to pay when they are broken: 'what oxytocin has joined together, let no man put asunder.' It takes much longer to unwind a bond's biological and emotional ties than it takes to form it in the first place. Human reactions to bereavement vary, of course, but the physical toll of grief is enough to elevate, for a time, the risk of heart disease and cancer.

So it's clear that the formation of close, stable, bonded relationships sits at the heart of our experience of being human. But what are we to make of it? At one level the answer is relatively simple: these biological processes have evolved because they have survival value. The vulnerability of the infant requires evolved mechanisms that attract, and then lock in, the attention of a devoted caregiver. In this evolutionary framework the entire landscape of human attraction – devotion, romance and self-giving altruism – is reduced to the survival chances that it confers.

I have no problem with recognizing the plausibility of this framework. It describes some of the mechanisms involved and how they may have developed. But is it the whole picture? Does it tell the entire story? I think there's much more going on than can be captured by a description of the physical mechanisms alone. The desire for relationships, for intimacy and affection, is fundamental to the purpose and meaning of our lives as creatures made in the image of God. We love like this because the One in whose image we are made loves like this. We are longing creatures because we long for him.

The end of longing

At the heart of the Christian understanding of God is his character as a relational being: Trinity – Father, Son and Holy Spirit. Bound in perfect trust, the three persons of the Trinity relate to one another in an eternal dance of love and self-giving. A few years ago, on a visit to Moscow, I went to see

Russia's most famous icon, *The Trinity*, by fifteenth-century painter Andrei Rublev.[5]

The Trinity depicts the Bible story about Abraham's three mysterious visitors at the Oak of Mamre (Genesis 18:1–33). If you look at the Genesis story, you will notice that as the conversation between Abraham and his guests unfolds, Abraham seems to be talking directly to God himself, and many people see a deeper reference to the life of the Trinity in the text at this point.

Looking at the icon more closely, you can discern its references to Father, Son and Holy Spirit too. The person on the left of the painting looks up towards the person in the centre, his hand a gesture of movement towards him. The person in the centre meets his gaze, apparently returning his love. But his body inclines towards the person on the right. This person, in turn, gazes over to the first person on the left, thus elegantly completing the relational circle.

But here's the point. The space they inhabit isn't triangulated to look inwards. It opens outward, towards you, the viewer. The table they sit around has four sides, but you, the viewer, are invited into the painting to fill the empty place.

Jesus taught us a great deal about the depth and intensity of love between the three persons of the Trinity. But this isn't an excluding love. As Jesus said, this is a love that invites us *in*:

> May they also be in us so that the world may believe that
> you have sent me. I have given them the glory that you gave
> me, that they may be one as we are one – I in them and you
> in me.
> (John 17:21–23)

Our desires, our most passionate longings, will only be fulfilled when we take our place at the table of God's love.

That is what our passionate longings are there for – to call us home. The writer of Ecclesiastes tells us that '[God] has also set eternity in the human heart' (Ecclesiastes 3:11). He's saying that the *whole person* is primed for, strains towards, longs for, our place at the table, our final union with God himself. And the movements of the eyes of a newborn child offer a first tantalizing glimpse of this eternal reality.

Human beings are thus fundamentally *lovers*. We are not primarily 'thinking beings', or even 'believing beings', but desiring agents made with a passionate orientation to a greater reality. As James K. A. Smith puts it,

> This is a structural feature of being human: we can't not be lovers; we can't not be desiring some kingdom. The question is not *whether* we love but *what* we love.[6]

'Our hearts are restless, until they can find their rest in you':[7] Augustine's famous words remind us that we can never be satisfied, at peace – never fully 'at home' – until we find our rest in him.

Sex life

So far, so good, but where does sex fit into all of this? If this is heading in the direction you are beginning to suspect it is heading, then it's all beginning to feel a bit uncomfortable. Are we talking about 'sex with God' here? We can't duck this question: if being human means being *ordered* towards God's love, how does our experience of *sexual* love – being attracted, aroused and experiencing sensuous pleasure – fit into this paradigm?

Let's begin by revisiting the sub-biblical roots of our discomfort. Most of us enter into early experiences of sexual arousal with a mixture of excitement and curiosity, fissured by powerful emotions of guilt and shame, emotions that will stick around for years to come. So talk of sexual feelings being a taster and picture of divine love brings those mixed emotions into play, leaving us feeling uncomfortable. We pay lip service to becoming entirely new creations in Christ, but the fig leaf remains firmly locked in place.

Over time we learn to have strained intellectual conversations about the relationship between sex and spirituality, provided they can be conducted in tones of deadly seriousness and a suitable furrowing of the brow. But at a gut level we keep the *emotions* that ripple through our experience of sex well clear of those that accompany our experience of God – in hermetically sealed compartments.

Perhaps we should be less surprised. If before all else we are desiring agents, made to be 'passionately orientated' towards God, we should expect our fractured and disordered loves to be slow to heal. Old habits die hard. But the gift of the sexual revolution to the church is to tell us that this is not good enough; it is forcing us to acknowledge the poverty of our body-denying pastoral theology. As James K. A. Smith puts it,

> A common 'churchy' response to this cultural situation runs along basically Platonic lines: to quell the raging passion of sexuality that courses its way through culture, our bodies and passions need to be disciplined by our 'higher' parts – we need to get the brain to trump other organs and thus bring the passions into submission to the intellect. And the way to do this is to get *ideas* to trump *passions*. In other words, the church responds to the overwhelming cultural activation and formation of desire by trying to fill our heads with ideas and beliefs . . . it's as if the church is pouring water on our heads to put out a fire in our heart.[8]

As we noted previously, secular culture understands the heart better than most Christians. We should thank God that the sexual revolution has stopped us in our tracks because it brings us face to face with our pastoral poverty and rubs our noses in it. And so, spurred on to seek something better, I'm going to ask my question again: if being fully human means that our loves are ordered towards God, how does our experience of *sexual* love – being attracted, aroused and experiencing sensuous pleasure – fit into this paradigm?

Sex God

The Bible portrays our relationship with God, and his with us, in a variety of images: a bear robbed of her cubs; a shepherd and his sheep; a lost son and his father; a king and his subjects; a woman and her mislaid coin; a friend who 'sticks closer than a brother'; a mother hen gathering her brood of chicks, and so on. These different images refract the kaleidoscopic range of passions that we have come to know as the mighty love of God.

But none of these images of God's love occurs with the frequency of the greatest picture of all – the union (including the sexual one-flesh union) of a husband and wife. The story of God's love begins in Genesis with a marriage between two people, and ends in Revelation with a marriage between Christ and his bride, the church. In between these two marriages the pages of the Bible rustle with images of love, betrothal, sex and marriage.

In the Old Testament God declares himself to be Israel's husband. Isaiah put it like this:

For your Maker is your husband –
the Lord Almighty is his name –

the Holy One of Israel is your Redeemer;
    he is called the God of all the earth.
(Isaiah 54:5)

And later he wrote,

as a bridegroom rejoices over his bride,
    so will your God rejoice over you.
(Isaiah 62:5)

Continuing with the theme of Israel as bride of the Lord, the prophets characterized Israel's idolatry as adultery. Their idolatry is nothing less than unfaithfulness to their spiritual husband, the Lord:

'But like a woman unfaithful to her husband,
    so you, Israel, have been unfaithful to me,'
                    declares the LORD.
(Jeremiah 3:20)

The emotional pain and anguish caused to God by Israel's unfaithfulness is compared with the feelings of a wronged partner who discovers his spouse has been having an affair.

Even leaving aside the entire book of the Song of Songs (as do the majority of preachers by the way), some of the most explicit use of sexual imagery is found in Ezekiel 16:8:

Later I passed by, and when I looked at you and saw
that you were old enough for love, I spread the corner
of my garment over you and covered your naked body.
I gave you my solemn oath and entered into a covenant
with you, declares the Sovereign LORD, and you became
mine.

Commentators rightly focus first on the tender generosity found in these verses. It's the story of how God rescues a newborn child abandoned in abject helplessness and poverty (verse 6), yokes himself to her in the covenant of marriage, and then beautifies and adorns her as a queen. But we mustn't airbrush the richly textured sexual imagery here: 'You grew and developed and entered puberty. Your breasts had formed and your hair had grown . . . and you became mine . . . I dressed you in fine linen and covered you with costly garments . . . adorned you with jewellery . . . earrings on your ears and a beautiful crown on your head' (verses 7–12).

What we are witnessing here is imagery of faithfulness yoked with passion. The marriage bond is about faithful love, yes. But Ezekiel won't settle for the sterile language of signing a marriage certificate: he wants the 'full Monty' – passion as well as faithfulness. So he paints a picture of the tender, sexualized, faithful desire that the marriage certificate frames. Ezekiel invites us to look into the world of our own sexual feelings: contemplate the shuddering oneness of consummation that follows the ceremony of married commitment. *This is what it is like.*

The imagery of bride and bridegroom threads its way through the New Testament too. Among the first titles used in the Gospels to describe Jesus is 'bridegroom' (Mark 2:19; John 3:29). And when Paul speaks of the one-fleshness of the sexual relationship between a husband and wife, he sees this as pointing us to the profound mystery of the intimate embrace of Christ and his church (Ephesians 5:30–32).

Looking in and looking along

These images make two important points about how we think about our sexuality, and specifically its *raw physicality*. First, the Bible has no problem comparing God's love with erotic human love. Eros captures the human experience of desire of such force and intensity that we feel almost physically compelled by it: the attraction of bottoms, breasts and torsos; the intense pleasures emanating from the vagina or penis that can crash through our bodies; the obsessive, near-delusional force of infatuation. If we want to understand God's love for us, we are invited to look into the most intimate and private corners of our felt sexuality and cross-refer.

Of course you may say, 'But this isn't quite me. I'm just not as sexually charged as other people seem to be.' Like so much else in life, the intensity and range of our sexual interests and experience lie on a spectrum, and it is perfectly natural to experience relatively low levels of sexual interest and desire. My point, however, is that when the Bible searches for pictures to help us comprehend the character and enormity of God's passion for us, it has no problems in embracing the entire spectrum of erotic desire. Of course elements of this are metaphorical – God is not embodied as we are – but in the Bible's portrayal of the intensity of the delight and pleasure that God feels towards us, it's as if nothing else but sex will do. So human erotic sexual desire is a picture of God's love, and we need to look *into* our sexuality to understand his love fully.

The second point is more important still. Besides looking 'into' our desires, we need to look 'along' them – much as we would look 'along' a signpost or the needle of a compass – to see where they point. It isn't simply the case that God's love for us is 'like' many aspects of our human sexual experience: our erotic experiences of being sexual point us towards God as well. They are a divine homing instinct for the glorious union that lies ahead. And he seeks from us the same faithful devotion, commitment, delight and joy that he, through

Christ, now finds in us. And, frankly, aspects of that love may feel, well . . . sexual.

(Key ideas in this chapter are grouped with those at the end of the next.)

14 THE END OF SHAME

How the biblical vision of sex confronts shame and puts the gospel on display

> These things – the beauty, the memory of our own past – are good images of what we really desire; but if they are mistaken for the thing itself they turn into dumb idols, breaking the heart of their worshippers. For they are not the thing itself; they are only the scent of a flower we have not found, the echo of a tune we have not heard, news from a country we have never yet visited. Do you think I am trying to weave a spell?[1]

Yes, Clive Staples Lewis, I think you were indeed trying to weave one of your spells. Since Lewis preached that great 'Weight of Glory' sermon in Oxford in 1941, the eyes of countless numbers have been opened to how the world of desire connects with the promise of heaven. Lewis believed that everyday objects of desire – a beautiful painting, a thrilling football match, the scent of a flower, a pulsating bassline played at full power – bring 'news from a far country'. These things summon us to 'come and behold' that great thing of which they are a faint and incomplete reflection. Lewis's friend Charles Williams coined the term 'romantic theology' for this experience. He even believed the thrill of coming across a rare and unique postage stamp could connect us with 'worship in the hidden temples of the Lord'.

Any occupation exercising itself with passion, with self-oblivion, with devotion, towards an end other than itself, is a gateway to divine things. If a lover contemplating in rapture the face of his lady, or a girl listening in joy to the call of the beloved, are worshippers in the hidden temples of our Lord, is not also the spectator who contemplates in rapture a batsman's stroke or the collector gazing with veneration at a unique example of a [postage stamp]?[2]

Stamp collecting? Tough one to imagine, but I can see what he was getting at.

But sex? Orgasms? Really?

Parts of the last chapter will have made uncomfortable reading for some. We are not used to mulling over how the world of raw sexual desire connects us with the stars. When we think about God, we are happy with the idea of platonic (spiritual, emotional) love, or agape (charitable, self-giving, compassionate) love. But erotic love? No thanks.

But this attitude towards the erotic is sub-biblical and it won't do. The gospel rescues all our longings – including our erotic desires – and brings them home. The Welsh talk about *hiraeth*, a strange, conflicted feeling of incompleteness, the boundless longing for a home from which we feel we have been exiled. Our erotic desires are looking for home too, and, as St Augustine reminds us, all our yearnings, every kind of longing, can find their full satisfaction only in God.

Full satisfaction: how sex anticipates God's passionate love

I recently read *The Divine Comedy*, Dante's epic poem written in the fourteenth century. It's a colourful allegory of life's journey, with a rich vein of Williams' romantic theology running through it.

The adventure begins with the poet lost in the dark wood of sin, and ends with his entry into paradise. When he finally arrives at the threshold of paradise, Dante encounters Beatrice, a woman he had first met in real life as a nine-year-old while living in Florence. He was rarely in her company after that, and in fact she died at the tender age of twenty-four, having been married to somebody else. For the rest of his life, however, Dante was besotted with his memory of Beatrice; what started as a childish crush became one of history's greatest stories of obsessive, unrequited love.

And yet here on the cusp of paradise, as Beatrice comes out to meet him, Dante can barely meet her gaze. In a gentle but firm reprimand, Beatrice tells us why. During his life, Dante had failed to *look along* his desires for her and allow them to find their true home.³ Further, before his devastating exile, as one of Florence's most powerful politicians, he had allowed his heart to be seduced by idolatries of money, sex and power. That is why he cannot look her in the eye. He knew he had lost his way.

But then, smiling, Beatrice welcomes him, and his longings for her, to their true home in God. And when he finally reaches out to the One who is the end of all desire, she simply disappears from view. Her work is over. Dante has found 'the thing itself' of which his love for her had been a pale reflection.

Jesus is my boyfriend?

A few years ago I helped to lead a men's ministry and gave a number of seminars about the challenges of reaching men with the gospel. Part of my routine involved sending up those mushy 'Jesus-is-my-boyfriend' songs. I enjoyed it. You know the scene – dreamy-eyed girl arrives late for the service, picks up a coffee at the back of church and slips into a faux ecstasy while singing 'I embrace you . . .' I argued that the erotic tone of these songs excludes men from sung worship because it sexualizes their relationship with Jesus. Our worship needs to be made of sterner stuff, I declared. Things had to change.

In fact, I was the one who needed to change. There may be good reasons for avoiding some of those songs, not least the dreary melody lines and their self-absorption, but fear of the erotic in human passion isn't one of them. James K. A. Smith hits the nail on the head again:

> I don't think we should so quickly write off [these songs'] 'romantic' or even 'erotic' elements (the Song of Songs comes to mind in this context) . . . While this can slide into an emotionalism and a certain kind of domestication of God's transcendence, there remains a kernel of 'fittingness' about such worship. While opening such doors is dangerous, I'm not sure that the primary goal of worship or discipleship is safety.[4]

So, in sum, drawing together the insights covered over these two chapters, there appear to be three main conclusions about the biblical understanding of sex and marriage.

Sexual desire teaches us about the intense passion of God's love

First, our sexual attractions and desires – our embodied experience – show us the passionate nature of God's love. We can learn about it in our heads, but the experience of our bodies brings it home to our hearts. Our 'pit-of-the-stomach' experience of desire, including the erotic tones of attraction and arousal, bear witness to, and direct us towards, the end of all longing in Jesus Christ. It's only a glimpse, of course. We mustn't mistake them for the real thing. We must not allow them to kindle further into lust, because that is sin. Yet it's the incompleteness of these earthy erotic experiences – the mistimed mutual orgasms, conflicted emotions, bored familiarity, unrequited love – that bears witness to the only true satisfaction for our longing. Our sexual interests are the teaser for the big movie yet to be released.

Both sex in marriage, and abstinence in singleness, showcase the faithful character of God's love

Second, sex is a picture of the faithful character of God's love. In the Bible sex is inextricably bound up with the covenant of marriage, presented to us as a permanent, 'for-better-for-worse', lifelong commitment of faithfulness. Similarly, God's love for us is also presented as faithful, covenantal and permanent: it doesn't waver; he doesn't do one-night stands; he doesn't grow tired of us; he doesn't 'fall in love' with somebody else. Marriage is an icon of God's faithfulness. And this great biblical institution puts this truth on display for all the world to see.

And so, as a couple make their wedding vows, they bear bodily witness to the covenantal character of God's love. Or rather, as they *keep* their wedding vows, they demonstrate its special character. A couple celebrating their wedding anniversary actually offer a stronger picture of God's love than a couple getting married. The essence of faithfulness is that it holds steady in the face of alternatives. Faithfulness is nurtured, tested and, in the end, strengthened by temptations. The wife and husband who remain faithful to each other – for richer or poorer, in sickness and in health – not only bear testimony to the kind of love that God has for us, but they put it on display. When did you last hear this spelled out in speech at a Christian golden wedding celebration?

But what about single people? It's important to grasp that single Christians who abstain from sex *outside* the marriage bond bear witness to the faithful nature of God's love with the same authority as those who have sex *inside* the marriage bond. Both paint pictures of God's faithfulness, but in different ways. Denying yourself something can be just as potent a picture of a thing's goodness as helping yourself to it.

Take the case of John the Baptist and Jesus. In Luke 7:33–34 Jesus vents his frustration with the scribes and Pharisees by reminding them that John the Baptist had come 'neither eating bread nor drinking wine', and they had accused him of having a demon. Jesus, in contrast, had come eating and drinking, and now they said, 'Here is a glutton and a drunkard, a friend of tax collectors and sinners.' But my point is that both behaviours pointed to the same reality: the coming kingdom of God. John's abstinence pointed forward to the coming of the Messiah when it would be the right time to feast; Jesus' behaviour proclaimed that the right time had now arrived. Both bore witness to the coming of the kingdom, but in different ways.

Similarly, both single and married people who abstain from sex outside the marriage bond point to the same thing. They both 'deploy' their sexuality in ways that serve as a sign of the kingdom and the faithful character of God's passion. In refusing to have sex outside marriage, the single person witnesses to the unbreakable link between passion and faithfulness. And in refusing to commit adultery, the married person bears witness to the same truth. This is an important point. I remember a single woman coming to me tearfully after a talk in which I was making this point. She wanted to tell me that for the first time in her life this insight had allowed her to see (and feel) that, despite her singleness, she was still a *sexual human being*. Single people who remain chaste so long as they are not married are not asexual. In fact, in their faithfulness to the sacred meaning of the marriage bond, their sexuality stands as a powerful witness to the true nature of God's faithful love. They point to a future reality in which we shall all be single in terms of human relationships, but 'married' in terms of our relationship with the Divine.

Singleness is a vocation for the Christian. Talking about a church that he pastored in central London, author Jonathan Grant makes the point that although the majority of members were single, very few had any sense of calling associated with their singleness:

> Many experienced their status as a burden, a wasteful holding pattern before finding someone and getting on with 'real' life. For many people singleness had become a strong *identity*, but one without any sense of *vocation*.[5]

If you are a single Christian, this won't do. Whether or not you will one day marry, your vocation now, in your body, is to bear witness to the faithful nature of God's passionate love.

Sex is a picture of the fruitful character of God's love

Third, our sexuality embodies the *fruitful* nature of God's love. The sex act, by its very nature, is open to the creation of new life, and the architecture of marriage sets in place the conditions that will nurture and develop that new life. In Genesis 1:27 the truth (which we saw earlier) that we are created in the image of God ('in the image of God he created them; male and female he created them') is followed immediately in verse 28 with perhaps its most creative expression: 'Be fruitful and increase in number.' Image-bearing produces more image-bearers. Of course not every marriage can bear children, for a host of different reasons, but that does not destroy its essential nature and orientation. Sex in marriage is open to children; it's shaped in the service of life.

These foundational verses in Genesis also tell us that God created human beings 'male and female'. The fruitfulness spoken of here can only be found in the complementary union of one man and one woman. No other form of sexual union has the potential to bear children. And no other union offers a full picture of the complementary nature of reconciliation – the coming together of earth and heaven, of God with his people, of Christ with his bride. That is why the biblical idea of marriage can't be re-engineered to validate other kinds of commitments, say between three people, or people of the same sex. In a secular society it is perfectly possible to enter into different types of civil contracts in such circumstances, but these kinds of arrangements are not the same thing as the biblical institution of marriage.

Life for the world?

There is one further strand to our understanding of the fruitful dimension of sex and marriage. So far our exploration of these themes has been largely individualistic in tone. There is a right and proper individualism, as we saw earlier: God calls us by name and meets our deepest and most personal desires for love. But the gospel vision of sex isn't individualistic in the sense that is driven by, and for, *my* needs. This is God's story that we are involved in, and our true freedom is found in learning to be his creatures and fulfilling his purposes. His call to us can never be individualistic in the sense of being narrowly focused on 'me' – *my* development and *my* well-being. The Christian vision for sex – whether we are married or single – is one of self-sacrifice for the common good. All the bees work together for the good of the whole hive.

This applies to our experience of erotic longing too. God calls us to order our passions in the service of a good greater than ourselves. Bringing children into the world and raising them in dedication to God is the most obvious expression of fruitfulness, but there are others too. Whether married or single, we are called to order our sexual interests in ways that support and nurture flourishing friendships, families and communities. This is the point at which the gospel vision pushes back hard against the secular narrative: it's about ordering our sex lives in the service of social justice, fairness and equality, serving the poor and the well-being of children, of life itself. So, to complete our brief journey through some of the big ideas of the Christian vision of sex and relationships, in the next chapter we will explore how the divine ordering of Eros is meant to serve God's big picture for human flourishing more generally.

Key ideas in chapters 13 and 14

- The Bible does not teach that there will be no marriage in heaven. Rather, it teaches there will be *one* marriage in heaven – between Christ and his bride, the church.
- When we 'look into' our sexual desires, we see the passionate nature of God's love for us. And when we 'look along' them, they point us to the reality that one

day all our longings, all our desires, will be fulfilled in the consummation of the marriage between Christ and his church.

- The biblical vision of sex breaks open three pivotal truths about God's love: it is passionate, always faithful and ultimately fruitful. As we allow the gospel to shape and discipline sexual desire, our lived bodily experience puts these truths on display. Just as passion and faithfulness go together in heaven, that's how it works here on earth too.

- Remaining chaste if we are single (whether for a part of, or all, our lives), and faithful to our vows if we are married, bears witness to the faithful character of God's love. Single people are not asexual. In their self-denial they too put God's faithful love on display in their body life. Single people also portray the truth that we shall all be single again one day as, finally, we are drawn into the ultimate consummation that takes place between Christ and his bride, the church.

15 FOR THE LIFE OF THE WORLD

How the biblical vision for sex and relationships opens the road to flourishing

So in the biblical vision Eros is ordered towards flourishing. But what exactly is 'flourishing'? Perhaps, like me, you think the word is so overused today that it risks having no meaning at all. But it's still a big, attention-grabbing word, and I think it's worth hanging on to. So before going any further, let's take a few moments to unpack how we understand it.

Flourishing is something to do with happiness and it's something to do with full satisfaction. But for our purposes, flourishing refers to what we see when the potential of a living thing is fully realized. Of course, depending on their worldview, people have very different pictures of what that potential looks like. For the Christian, however, to flourish is to realize the full potential of what it means to be created and redeemed in the image of God. It is to realize our identity in Christ. To fully, freely, wholly live out who we are – to God's glory.

Part of our potential as divine image-bearers involves the development of human creativity, our God-given ability to make more of the world into which God has placed us. We flourish by being fruitful, and a big part of that, as we've seen, is the creation and nurture of new life. But there are other registers of human creativeness too: we have learned how to turn wheat into spaghetti, how to manufacture antibiotics out of fungus and how to send people into space. Another part of bearing the divine image involves the development of character. We flourish as we show more of the fruit of the Spirit: being 'in Christ' is about being like him and becoming more like him.

Flourishing and human relationships

There's also a relational dimension to flourishing and, in the Christian understanding, we cannot overstate its importance. God's nature is to be relational because his nature *is* relational. In Genesis, God doesn't say, 'I am going to make mankind in my image', but rather, 'Let *us* make mankind in *our* image, in *our* likeness' (Genesis 1:26). The full doctrine of the Trinity unfolds only gradually, but this early reference to God's relational nature sets the record straight right from the beginning: God is not a distant deity dwelling in splendid isolation.

Author Dale S. Kuehne reminds us,

> Relationships . . . are not a product of his creation; they are part of God's very nature. It is for this reason that the concept 'God is love' makes sense. Since he is relational by nature, God knows love because God lives love in the Trinity.[1]

Clearly, God's relational image affects the way we think about working out our identity as God's image-bearers: we are incomplete without others, and made for fulfilment in relationship with each other. Look how Jesus wanted his followers to enjoy the wholeness in their relationships that he and his Father already enjoyed:

> My prayer is not for them alone. I pray also for those who will believe in me through their message, that all of them may be one, Father, just as you are in me and I am in you. May they also be in us so that the world may believe that you have sent me. (John 17:20–21)

Flourishing and the glory of God

Lastly, the biblical picture of flourishing isn't a self-fulfilment project. That would be a travesty of its real meaning. *Look along* true, godly flourishing, and you see the glory of God. That is what flourishing is for. In fact, because the 'glory and honour of the nations will be brought into it' (Revelation 21:26), the New Jerusalem is the home of all godly ambition and flourishing. Do you grasp the beauty of this verse? It says that all the creative splendours of the nations – their best architecture, their mighty feats of engineering, their greatest art and most inspiring literature – will be paraded into the New Jerusalem because *the glory of God is where they belong*. So true flourishing is a gift from God and, in the end, returns glory and honour back to him.

So far, so good. But *how* do we flourish? And, more specifically, what does it mean for our sexuality to be ordered towards flourishing in this way?

Flourishing and the law of consequences

Our first task is to grasp where the idea of flourishing sits within the broader relationship between God's sovereignty and human responsibility. On the one hand, the potential for, and the experience of, flourishing is ultimately a gift of God's grace. It is freely given and unearned. At the same time, flourishing is a part of our human responsibility and subject to the biblical law of consequences. These two insights have to be held in tension: God moves towards us in grace, and all that we accomplish is in his strength and grounded in his sovereign purpose; at the same time, we are held responsible for hearing God's Word and then doing it. And when we fail to respond to God's Word, we must be prepared to face the consequences.

Human flourishing is tied to human obedience and the law of consequences. We see this principle at work in both the Old and New Testaments. From Israel's founding as a nation, for example, God makes clear that his people have been brought out of Egypt by his mighty hand alone. But then he spells out how the law of consequences would govern their national life:

> See, I set before you today life and prosperity, death and
> destruction. For I command you today to love the LORD
> your God, to walk in obedience to him, and keep his
> commands, decrees and laws; then you will live and increase,
> and the LORD your God will bless you in the land you are
> entering to possess.
> (Deuteronomy 30:15–16)

Moral obedience and flourishing would go together like a horse and cart. Flourishing for the Israelites ('living' and 'increasing') would follow naturally from walking in God's ways. It would depend on the choices they made and the actions they pursued.

This principle spills over into the New Testament too. After setting out the great doctrines of free grace in his letter to the

Galatians, Paul goes on to warn his readers that 'a man reaps what he sows ' (Galatians 6:7).

Of course, God is a God of forgiveness and compassion. Over and over, when we turn to him in repentance, he freely forgives us our sins. He sometimes graciously delivers us from the consequences of our actions too. But while we can count on God's grace for forgiveness, we can't count on being shielded from all the consequences of our poor choices and sinful actions. I think of pastors caught up in sexual misconduct: despite the free forgiveness of God's grace, nobody can undo the consequences for their ministry or the wreckage in the lives of countless ordinary Christians whose confidence in the gospel has been shattered by the abuse of their trust.

But we mustn't focus on the negative example of the law of consequences. The big narrative of the Bible, the main road of its promises, resonates with positive images. For those who walk in God's ways, the pages of Scripture rustle with pictures of fruitfulness, justice, prosperity and shalom: 'Do this and you will *live*':

> Then the Lord your God will make you most prosperous in
> all the work of your hands and in the fruit of your womb, the
> young of your livestock and the crops of your land. The LORD
> will again delight in you and make you prosperous, just as he
> delighted in your ancestors.
> (Deuteronomy 30:9)

But hold on. You don't need to browse a newspaper for very long to come across examples of obedience rewarded with suffering, and devil-may-care lifestyles rewarded with fabulous wealth. That is why Job was so perplexed: if God keeps his promises, why had his life swerved so disastrously off-piste?

It was the same sense of betrayal that fuelled the psalmists' anguished protests about the prosperity of the wicked. What had gone wrong with the law of consequences?

Flourishing and the long view

The promise of flourishing operates in the 'big picture' of God's sovereignty. Only God sees the whole. He works to a different timeline from ours, and his promises are sometimes realized generations later. Also, many of the biblical promises of flourishing were made to whole communities, rather than to individuals. We mustn't take the promises of national prosperity and flourishing made during the Old Testament era and map them over simplistically to our personal circumstances today. Finally, God is interested in character much more than achievement and material prosperity. Paul wanted the Ephesians to 'become mature, attaining to the whole measure of the fulness of Christ' (Ephesians 4:13). God works to bring Christlikeness to our hearts, not money to our bank balances. That is his vision of flourishing over the long term.

Nevertheless, there is still an important principle at work here: in the *long run*, walking in God's ways, being obedient to his moral law, leads to life in all its fullness – personal, relational and cultural. We have become experts in the consequences of disobedience ('don't do that, you'll go blind!'), but if we want to win hearts and minds with a truly biblical vision of sex and relationships, we need to recover the positive biblical promise of flourishing too.

But how does this happen? Specifically, what part does our sexuality, including the ordering of our erotic desires, play in serving this greater good of human flourishing? In the biblical vision, human flourishing is delivered through two of God's greatest gifts: the institutions of the family and the church. These are the God-given means by which human sexuality is ordered towards grace-drenched flourishing.

Flourishing and the gift of institutions

Uh? Did I say institutions? 'The gospel vision for sex and relationships offers . . . er, institutions.' Hardly an idea to get the pulse racing and set the imagination on fire. Institutions bring to mind pictures of decaying Victorian lunatic asylums, tradition-bound churches and faceless banking conglomerates. So what do I mean by the gift of institutions?

In fact, any persisting pattern of organized human behaviour is effectively *an institution*. At their best, institutions cradle the wisdom that has been accumulated over several generations and help to carry it forward into the future. They set up social frameworks and structures that conserve the best ideas of the past, so that they don't have to be reinvented with each new generation.

Take the example of higher education, an institution I worked in for much of my life. Over the years new teaching methods were introduced, buildings were demolished, and staff came and went. And yet, even though the mode of delivery changed dramatically, the central vision of nurturing education and the skills to deliver it rolled on. The values and goals of higher education had become deeply embedded in long-term patterns of human behaviour. And so, understood in this organic, relational sense, institutions curate the wisdom that is necessary to nourish and sustain flourishing.

But there are bad as well as good institutions and, in recent years, instances where malpractice and corruption have become institutionalized have generated growing public mistrust. This, taken together with the cult of the individual we discussed earlier, means that many institutions have gone into decline, particularly those of an intermediate size.

You can think of institutions as operating at three levels. The smallest are those that affect our immediate social world, such as marriage or, in church groups, a small Bible study group or prayer triplet. Macro-level institutions are those of government, the civil service, the NHS, and so on. Increasingly, our macro-level relationships are also being institutionalized electronically in the social media world of Facebook and Twitter. Here you may easily find yourself part of a framework of several hundred friends on Facebook and a couple of thousand followers on Twitter. Intermediate-sized institutions sit somewhere in-between, for example in local community organizations, scouts and guides, rotary clubs, a local church and the extended family network.

The brunt of the decline of recent years has in fact been borne by *intermediate-level institutions*. On either side, micro- (groups of friends who meet up regularly in the pub after work on Fridays) and macro-sized institutions continue to thrive (especially virtual institutions such as Facebook). So what's the problem? Why should we care about the decline of inter-mediate institutions? The problem is that at the micro-personal and the macro-social level we generally only need tolerate people so long as we choose to associate with them. You can stop going to the pub after work if you don't like somebody, or you can unfriend an objectionable character on social media. But when it's this easy, our personal networks can become self-serving and narcissistic, because we tend to prefer people who are like us. There is much less scope for the kind of character development that comes from seeing relation-ships through over the long haul, and among a wider variety of personality types. And yet these are precisely the kinds of relationships that figure in intermediate-sized organizations.

Character development is a particular virtue of inter-mediate communities because they contain a broader mix of personality types and force us to work out our relational conflicts over the long term, often through having to cooperate around some common interest or cause. And that is why their decline, coupled with the rise of individualism, is potentially so problematic for human flourishing. The biblical vision, however, presents us with two major institutions of the inter-mediate type – the extended family and the local church – and calls us to discipline our sexuality and relationships in ways that support and sustain them. In turn, these institutions help us to do that. So the gift of these two intermediate institutions creates a virtuous circle of character development and moral formation. Let's take family first.

The institution of the family

The family is the oldest, most recognizable and most durable institution in history. Everybody is born into a family. The family is a gift of God's common grace, by which he 'causes his sun to rise on the evil and the good, and sends rain on the righteous and the unrighteous' (Matthew 5:45). It's for everybody.

As a tool for building strong, tested, mature relationships, nothing promotes human flourishing like the extended family. Think about how challenging family relationships are. You are flung together with a wide range of different people over a lifetime. Their views and decisions impact on your education, your life and your loves. You have to negotiate relationships across the boundaries of age, sex and (sometimes) ethnicity. And your options for picking the temperament and personality of those journeying with you in this lifelong stress-incubator are extremely limited.

Then think how joyful and fulfilling family relationships can be: the laughter of children; the opportunity to create and nurture new life; the satisfaction of seeing youngsters grow and begin to flourish; the knowledge that when the chips are down and you need help, you'll get all the support, love and affection you need; opportunities to pool resources, share visions and pursue dreams together. The list of potential blessings is endless.

Given the agony and the ecstasy of family life, can you think of a better crucible for the development of godliness? Of course, our hopes and aspirations are scrambled by divorce and separation, by sickness and death. In a fallen world the promised blessings of children are torpedoed by infertility. And family feuding can be vicious and destructive. But the fact that we fall short of these ideals, and find these commitments so challenging, doesn't mean they should be abandoned. There may be a thousand exceptions, but it's still a good rule: overall, in the round, we flourish as human beings when we see through the commitments that come with families. And there can be no more important commitment than the one we make to children.

Christianity's revolution of childhood

We have forgotten just how deep a cultural revolution was brought about by the way early Christians treated their children. In his book *When Children Became People* church historian O. M. Bakke reminds us that before the coming of Christianity, children were considered to be virtually non-persons in much of Greek and Roman culture.[2] In the strict social hierarchy of the time freeborn adult males were at the top of the pack, and women, slaves and children at the bottom. One of its most chilling practices was *expositio* – the abandoning of unwanted children to die or be 'rescued' into slavery. Thus, in Rome, brothels specializing in child sex slaves were legal, thriving public enterprises, and the wealthy also had the right to treat their child slaves in any way they chose:

> Suetonius [the Roman historian] condemns Tiberius because he 'taught children of the most tender years, whom he called his little fishes, to play between his legs while he was in the bath. Those which have not yet been weaned, but were strong and hearty, he set at fellatio.' . . . The decisive point is not the degree of truth there may be in this story but the fact that Suetonius clearly thought his readers would find it credible. Brothels staffed by boys existed in many towns. Intercourse with castrated boys is often described as especially exciting, and we know that babies were castrated so that they could work in brothels later on. One reason why people bought small children as slaves was in order to have sex with them.[3]

This was the world into which Christianity was born, but Christians immediately adopted a radically different approach to the way they loved and cared for their children. Why were they so passionate about them? Because they remembered how God's anger burned against the Israelites caught up in child sacrifice. They remembered how Jesus called children to him and put them at the very heart of his vision of what the kingdom of heaven looks like. They remembered how Jesus instructed his followers to imitate children and find ways to become like them. These were the convictions that turned Greek and Roman culture upside down.

In the face of the injustices and inequalities heaped upon them by the sexual revolution, children need to be right back at the centre of our vision for the family. Church leaders in the UK rightly call upon governments to do more for children by alleviating child poverty or improving educational opportunities. But in a culture where fully one-half of children reach maturity with only one parent in the home, the most important intervention they could make would be to set out more clearly a compelling case for the social goods of marriage and family.

The institution of the family and you

Now you may be thinking, 'I'm twenty-two, single, and unlikely to be married for several years. I take your point about families and children, but what's in it for me? What does the institution of the family have to do with me and my sexuality right now?'

First, your default response reflects just how far our culture has captured your heart. This is radical individualism at work. The point is that God is calling you now to curate your sexuality in the service of life, for human flourishing generally. You are not your own, but you (including your erotic desires) have been bought with a price. One of the ways you support the family right now is by honouring the covenant of marriage, the bedrock of the family, with your chastity. As we saw earlier, your faithful abstinence from sex outside marriage is just as powerful a statement of the unbreakable link between covenant and intimacy as that offered by marriage itself.

Second, everybody has a stake in seeing families thrive. You were born into a family. Your experiences of family have been shaped by the choices and commitments of the networks of people that have gone before you. Now it's your turn to support families in your sexual abstinence, and your wider community participation, which I'll amplify momentarily.

Third, and finally, the children in your fellowship are part of your responsibility too. So give them support by honouring the institution that cares for them and by doing all you can – helping in crèche, toddler groups, youth groups, babysitting

– to support them. Preserving and nourishing the institution of the family is a task that involves all of us, because when families flourish, we all do.

The institution of the church

Let's turn now to the second great institution revealed by the Christian vision: the local family of the church. There are two ways of joining a family: you are born into one or you are adopted into one. Through the gospel we do both. We are born into earthly families, but also adopted into the wider family (or, better, the 'household') of God. And the household of God, the family of the local church, is just about as perfect an example as you will find of those 'intermediate-level' community organizations that, over the past few decades, have been in free fall elsewhere in society.

As we have seen, intermediate-sized communities expose us to people and personality types we might otherwise avoid. Being assigned by your church to a small group is a good example of people who would otherwise be unlikely to socialize together being flung into one another's company. It can be hard going. But sharing community in this way gives you the opportunity to develop empathy, learn compassion and build solidarity. Many readers will have had the experience of finding themselves placed in a home group with somebody they don't know particularly well but have always found slightly difficult. And yet as you have got to know them, you have found yourself becoming more tolerant, affectionate even, towards them.

But what does the biblical vision for sex and marriage have to do with flourishing local churches? Besides being obedient to the foundational truths that bind together the whole fellowship, the biblical vision anchors the families that make up such a large and important part of the life of a local church community. And families flourish when they play a full part in these intermediate-sized communities too. The gospel's vision is of families with flexible outer boundaries, involving their children in creative hospitality, and together serving the poor and the needy (Romans 12:13; Hebrews 13:2; 1 Peter 4:9).

Single Christians and the community of the church
The importance of single people to the life of the wider spiritual family of the church cannot be overstated. Here they become spiritual mothers and fathers, brothers and sisters, sons and daughters. Paul, a single man, treated Timothy as a son and experienced powerful fatherly emotions towards him. Similarly, Lydia, who appears to have been a single woman, ran a business from a household large enough to host a church as well. She used her home to show hospitality to visitors, including offering Paul and Silas a place to stay after their discharge from prison. In fact, Lydia provides one of the most inspirational examples of how the Christian vocation of singleness can reverberate in a full and fruitful life of commerce, hospitality, godly leadership and gospel ministry.

This calls for an explicit, intentional engagement with the idea of the Christian single life as a vocation. Single people should not be tagged on to families, but should seek to become more integral to them, providing wisdom and skills, helping buffer against inward-looking selfishness. And no matter how limited resources may be, the single vocation offers the chance to build a home, perhaps by becoming part of an extended household with other singles, and offering hospitality to married couples, whole families, even.

Of course, I recognize the idealism in these aspirations, but thank God that the sexual revolution is forcing us to get to grips with this. I think of a church nearby with a network of community-living homes in which single Christians serve along with married couples and families. That is one idea. Then I think of Tony, a single, middle-aged man who works as a delivery van driver on the minimum wage. His home is a creative, warm and generous oasis of hospitality for other members of his church. That is another example. There is no one-size-fits-all for integrating both single and married people into a flourishing local church, but that is the task that lies ahead of us.

Flourishing and society

Finally, what about wider society? Does the biblical vision of sex, marriage and relationships have anything to say about human flourishing beyond the church? In the book of Jeremiah the prophet writes to console the Jews who have been taken as captives into exile (Jeremiah 29 – 33). He starts with the good news: one day they are going to return to their beloved land. God is going to make a new covenant with them, one written on their hearts. But then comes the bad news. They need to dig in for a long stay. Jeremiah counsels them to build houses to live in, plant gardens and allow their families to flourish. And then he says this:

> Also, seek the peace and prosperity of the city to which I have carried you into exile [says the Lord]. Pray to the Lord for it, because if it prospers, you too will prosper.
> (Jeremiah 29:7)

It's an astonishing instruction. The enslaved are supposed to pray for the enslavers, to cheer for them, to seek their welfare, to invest in their well-being and peaceableness. Of course, there is a degree of self-interest here ('because if it prospers, you too will prosper'), but this summons connects directly with Jesus' command to his followers to live as salt and light (Matthew 5:13–16). We are called alongside our neighbours, praying, and working, for their peace and well-being, loving them in word and action.[4] That is why you will find Christians on the streets on Saturday nights, helping intoxicated people find their way home, or combatting human trafficking, providing shelter for the homeless, or taking care of the sick. Christians have always been at the forefront of compassionate social endeavour.

It's time to recover our confidence that the Christian vision for sex, marriage and family also conveys social and relational goods that can bring blessing and flourishing to all. We need to be ready to share what we ourselves have found to be true for the sake of children in need, because a culture of strong marriages brings stability to their emotional and psychological development, alleviates poverty and enhances educational outcomes, and to do so for the sake of the poor more generally too, because it is they who bear the brunt of the collapse of marriage. We do it for the sake of women, because the Christian vision of men who love their wives as Christ loves the church condemns outright the abuses of psychological control and aggression, and for the sake of young men, because in the Christian vision their days of being Peter Pan are numbered. And we need to share what we have found, for the sake of all whose lives have been hollowed out by pornography, promiscuity, trafficking, and by the fruitless pursuit of self-fulfilment. We have been given life for the world and we cannot keep it to ourselves.

We shall need to open a new chapter in the history of Christian apologetics, making our case in reasoned debate and by the careful use of evidence from the social sciences. We can also support the work of think tanks and pressure groups that advocate in these areas: in the UK, for example, through the work of the Marriage Foundation or organizations such as CARE. In our local churches we can offer mums and toddlers groups, father and son ventures, parenting classes and marriage courses, open to all and serving the community around us.

In sum, we do all this because we love people, and especially children, the poor and the weak. The genius of Martin Luther King Jr in fighting racism lay in his vision of justice for all. King argued that in fighting for justice, blacks were not fighting for themselves, but for everybody: 'Injustice any- where is a threat to justice everywhere. We are caught in an inescapable network of mutuality tied in a single garment of destiny.'[5]

This must be our vision too. We must be prepared to defend and advocate for these ways of life not because they are good for ourselves, but because they are good for everybody. In the past we tried to impose them by law. Now, thanks to the revo- lution, we must demonstrate their plausibility in the authentic reality of our lives. That is the only convincing way we will be able to tell a better story.

And that, as we near the end of our journey, is the final task that lies ahead. What is our story? And how will it be better than the failed promise of the revolution?

Key ideas in this chapter

- In the Christian worldview flourishing is about realizing our potential as human beings made in the image of God. It's about becoming fruitful, creative and relational human beings, alongside the development of Christlike character.

- Moral obedience and human flourishing are bound together by the biblical law of consequences. Given our limited perspective in a fallen world, at an individual level the link isn't always visible. In the long run, however, the principle is clear. We need to recover our confidence in God's promise that obedience leads to abundant life. Obedence and self-sacrifice do not diminish us, but rather open the road to true freedom.
- Human flourishing is served by God's gifts of the institutions of the extended family and the local church. These two institutions carry the knowledge of God's ways down through the generations, and everybody – single and married, young and old – has a stake in supporting and nurturing them.
- Children have paid the price massively for the failed promise of the sexual revolution, and these institutions are especially powerful in serving their needs and protecting their interests.
- The institutions of the family and the local church must never become self-serving and inward-looking. They have a crucial role in fulfilling the Christian vocation of bringing life to the whole world.

16 OUR BETTER STORY

Crafting a narrative for hearts as well as minds

Over the past few chapters we have drawn together some of
the main ideas, facts and themes that together make up the
Christian vision for sex and relationships. As we prepare now
to craft some kind of narrative, let's summarize where we've
got to under three broad headings:

Identity and learning to be God's creatures and image-bearers

- The Christian vision for sex and relationships is
  grounded in the foundational truth that human beings
  are creatures made in the image of God. Our identity
  is defined by this reality. It isn't something that we
  have discovered within ourselves or constructed for
  ourselves – our Creator revealed it to us.
- Although sin has disfigured and distorted the image
  of God in human beings, Christ's death and resurrection
  have made possible its full restoration. As we trust in

him, and live and work towards the final restoration
of all things in him, the process of renovation is already
well under way.

- Living out our God-given identity as divine image-
bearers puts us on the road to a flourishing that
involves fruitful, creative endeavour and a
transformation of our relationships – including
our sexual relationships.

Sex and the divine image

- Sexual feelings and bodily desires are an important
part of what it means to bear God's image, and we
flourish as we bring them into harmony with our
God-given identity. Our sexual longings are a
homing instinct for the Divine, pointing us to the
only intimate union that fully satisfies – the one with
God himself.
- As divine image-bearers, we are called to love in the
same way that God loves. Because God's intimate love
for us is bound up with faithfulness and fruitfulness,
that is how we express our most intimate level of love
for each other as well – in a relationship of faithfulness
and fruitfulness called marriage. This form of bodily
expression of our sexuality also puts the story of
God's love on display to the world.
- Marriage is a gift from God – a sacred covenant
between one man and one woman that paints a
vivid picture of Christ's love for his church. Both the
married (by their faithfulness) and the unmarried (by
their chastity) play their different roles in upholding
the biblical concept of marriage as the only God-given
context for intimate sexual love.

Flourishing as God's image-bearers

- For Christians, true human flourishing isn't found in the pursuit of self-fulfilment, but in living in harmony with our true identity. It involves playing our part in the bigger story of the break-in of God's rule; we flourish when we look outwards, serving others and working for a good greater than ourselves.
- Two God-given institutions – the family and the local church – play a central role in nourishing this big, inclusive vision of human flourishing, and strong marriages have an integral part in both. These relational networks provide mutual support, help build and develop character, and ensure stable and protective environments for children.
- All Christians, regardless of age, marital state, gender or sexuality, by living faithfully in harmony with their identity in Christ, are called to play their part in supporting these two life-giving institutions. The biblical vision for sex is a holistic one in which everybody lives self-sacrificially for the common good.
- Making sacrifices for this greater good is tough in today's culture of entitlement. Living in harmony with your Christian identity is especially challenging for those struggling in unhappy marriages or those experiencing bisexual or same-sex attraction. We remain firm in our convictions, however, because, in the long run, this Christian vision brings flourishing for the many as well as the few.
- Nobody has ever kept these ideals of marriage, sex and family as they should. Christian communities are places of sin, failure and struggle, as well as of hope and grace. And so Christians are called to work to build accepting

communities that offer support and compassion to all, regardless of background or circumstance.
- We believe that these ways of life, rooted in our Christian identity, are not only good for us, but that they are good for everybody. They help build stronger communities and protect the most vulnerable of all – our children and the poor.

Putting our story together

These are important principles and statements, but, as we've seen, there is a difference between making statements and casting a narrative. So how can we weave together a narrative to win hearts and minds?

We must start by recognizing the naivety of believing that, even with the most compelling narrative, this vision will be welcomed in the public square. No matter how winsome, how persuasive, our case, no matter how well we manage to prove its life-giving goodness, standing against the flow always courts rejection. We are fallen, prideful creatures who do not welcome the exposure of sin in our lives. No matter how well we avoid being judgmental, people *will* feel judged and resentful. That is why Jesus told us to take up our cross and follow him. Equally, we cannot forget that this is a clash of moral vision: we can't prevent those with different concepts of goodness and flourishing from finding offence, danger even, in what we profess. But for the life of the world, for the sake of the gospel, we cannot remain silent. This is the challenge that lies ahead.

So what might our narrative begin to look like?

In chapter 5 we identified the three hallmarks of the sexual revolution's narrative as heroic individualism, a redemptive trajectory and a clear moral vision. This is our starting point.

Our narrative must also connect with the individualistic, compassion-driven morality of today's culture, while managing to communicate something about the importance of the big principles that safeguard the many as well as the few. In other words, we must try to communicate our conviction that it is no use catering for the needs of a minority of bees if in doing so we destroy the whole hive. Finally, our narrative needs to engage with today's moral concerns about equality, injustice and freedom from oppression.

So, using this simple structure as our starting point, perhaps our narrative could begin to look something like the one shown in the panel here:

The huge changes wrought by the sexual revolution over the past few decades have made us think long and hard about what we really believe. We realize that we had often allowed a deficient, sub-Christian view of sex to dominate our communities and shape our attitudes. This made us look harsh and judgmental, and many people felt diminished and excluded. And rather than serving the vulnerable and poor, our moral convictions were sometimes used as weapons to beat them over the head.

The sexual revolution has been a wake-up call for us, and we want to turn back from these failures. The revolution has challenged us to acknowledge, and deal with, the shame we feel about our sexuality, and we owe it a debt of gratitude.

But as time passes by, it's becoming ever more clear that the sexual revolution has failed as well. Far from having more and better sex, people's sex lives are as confused today as they ever have been. The retreat from marriage has affected the poorest communities most seriously, heaping injustice on the vulnerable and especially our children. The pornographication and sexualization of childhood is a tragedy unfolding before our eyes. Modern confusion over questions of identity has left a frightening emptiness at the centre of what it means to be human and, looking to the future, nobody seems to know what the end game will be.

Faced with these realities, we have rediscovered our vision for sex and marriage, a vision rooted in the Big Story of God's love for the world. As Christians today, we come in all shapes and sizes, different sexualities and from all kinds of ethnic backgrounds. But our real story begins with our name – Christians. For us, identity isn't something we discovered within ourselves, or something shaped by our ever-changing culture; it is something that God has given us. Our Christian identity is a sacred gift, and we have discovered that we flourish as human beings when we live in harmony with who we really are.

Our vision for sex and relationships is as tough and demanding today as it ever has been, but we are discovering that it's often the hard choices that lead to something solid and lasting. We believe God loves us passionately. And because his love is always permanent and faithful, for Christians, sexual intimacy is always bound up in the faithful commitment of marriage between one man and one woman too. This is the shape of life to which God calls us, and we are finding that living in harmony with our Christian identity helps build stronger families and communities, and protects our children and the most vulnerable.

And so for Christians, sex is a sacred part of our identity, and we don't think you can pick and choose. We recognize these ideals are especially hard for those who are unable to be married or who struggle in unhappy marriages. But true compassion serves the needs of the many as well as the few, and we are convinced that this sacred link between sex and marriage offers the best chance of flourishing for all. And we are inspired and energized by the countless women and men in our communities who are sacrificially living out their identities to serve the common good.

We don't want to repeat the mistakes of the past. While we can't stop advocating for ways of life that we believe bring flourishing, we won't try to impose them again, because people must be free to make their own choices. Instead, regardless of circumstances or background, we want to invite anyone and everyone to join us in this adventure and prove it for themselves.

Well, that's my first attempt at a better story. You may think it's not a particularly good one. You may already be thinking of ways whereby you could reshape it into something better. I hope so. Because your story needs to be *your story*. If we think about the power of stories simply as a strategy to win arguments, then we are doomed to fail. Our narrative needs to be grounded in conviction and told with genuine passion. It needs to come from the heart – your heart. So, as you think about the work that lies ahead, bear these two points in mind.

You have to believe your story

You can't hover around the edge of this question for ever. If you want to tell a better story, you have to believe it yourself. I have already emphasized that this book isn't written to convince you about the authority of the Bible. I'm talking about a deeper level of formation of its teaching here. I'm challenging you to ask whether you yet hold these beliefs with the level of conviction that will fuel your passion for them.

The UK Parliament votes by 'dividing'. Literally. Members of Parliament have to leave their seat and walk in one of two directions: those who want to vote 'yes' pass through a 'division lobby' to the right, and those voting 'no' make their way through the lobby on the left. As a Member of Parliament, you can't keep your opinions to yourself. There's no secret ballot booth. Getting up from your seat, pushing against the flow, you have to nail your colours to the mast in the most public way possible. Responsible government of a nation means that you not only 'talk the talk', you need to 'walk the walk' as well – literally, by making your way through the voting lobbies.

Our convictions do not always have to be demonstrated so publicly. There is a time to act and a time to remain silent. What we cannot compromise on, however, is the need to make up our minds about these weighty issues. For the sake of our young people, for the poor and vulnerable, we can't continue sitting on the fence for ever.

'You like to-may-toes'

But you may protest, 'You like to-may-toes and I like to-mah-toes' – why can't we all just get along? As we face the challenges of poverty, climate change and the big questions of social justice, doesn't getting bogged down in sex simply play the devil's game? Can't we just get along while holding a diversity of views?

I really don't think we can. The Bible tells us that sex is much more than a bit player in God's big picture. The experience of desire (and sexual desire is possibly the most powerful and repercussive of human desires) sits at the core of what it means to be human. In God's economy immoral behaviour is viewed as sinful, abhorrent and incompatible with inheriting his kingdom (1 Corinthians 6:9). So figuring out the boundaries of what constitutes moral behaviour is at the heart of godly formation.

It's tempting to think that we can simply pick and mix from God's moral law, depending on the contingencies of culture. But the biblical vision for sex is like a sweater with a loose thread hanging out: if you pull at it, eventually the whole thing unravels. And don't be fooled by accusations of simplistic or 'fundamentalist' approaches to Scripture. The orthodox case is grounded in the best traditions of biblical interpretation and hermeneutics.[1]

And neither must we allow those who accuse orthodox Christians of being obsessed with sex (while clearly being obsessed themselves) to shame us. Sex is important and can wreak fearful destruction. A roll call of otherwise perfectly rational and reasonable people – including well-known pastors and leading politicians – have tragically trashed their families and wrecked their careers for a night of it. Courageous men and women march in Gay Pride parades, through some of the most bigoted and dangerous neighbourhoods in the world, to defend their right to it. And the emotional scars that disfigure the lives of thousands of children who have been taken into care from broken homes bear witness to its power to destroy. And so, far from being a personal matter, issues of sex and the ordering of sexual relationships sit at the heart of God's big picture for the life of the world.

There's more intellectual spadework ahead. A number of issues surrounding, say, the nature and meaning of same-sex attraction and gender dysphoria lie beyond the scope of this book, but you will find suggestions for further reading at the end.

You need to live your story

There is more to believing our story than getting the intellectual framework in place. How do we reach beyond the intellect to influence and change the deeper places of the heart? Going back to our elephant metaphor, how do we get the elephant to change direction as well as the rider? The elephant is a creature of habit with a long memory. We have plenty of information to instruct the rider, but how do we move the elephant?

Believing is seeing

First, you need to fire the imagination. The elephant is moved by emotion and imagination. One of C. S. Lewis's greatest gifts has been to inspire evangelically minded Christians to rediscover their imaginations. We return to his 'Weight of Glory' sermon, and see this illustration:

> It is a serious thing to live in a society of possible gods and goddesses, to remember that the dullest and most uninteresting person you can talk to may one day be a creature which, if you saw it now, you would be strongly tempted to worship, or else a horror and a corruption such as you now meet, if at all, only in a nightmare. All day long we are, in some degree, helping each other to one or other of these destinations.[2]

You have heard the phrase 'live with the end in mind', but here Lewis shows us how the end can fire your imagination in ways that will help you to do that. But what does this mean for the biblical approach to sex? It starts with how you think about your body. Look at yourself. The image of God in your body is broken in disrepair, but the process of renovation has already started from the inside out. Your body is holy, wonderful and sacred. One day it will be made completely new. It has been sending you homing signals since your earliest sexual awakening, and God has broken into your life to say, 'honour me with your body', and let its longing bring you home.

When you see a single person, what do you *see*? Do you see how their chaste, graceful movements honour God with every step they take? Do you see how their faithfulness to the gospel challenges married couples to stay faithful as well?

When you see a young couple walking hand in hand, look *along* what you see, and ask, where is this pointing? Why is it happening? What does it mean? You can start to exercise your imagination now. Try it. We must challenge our church leaders too, to feed their sheep once again by firing their imagination with what the gospel makes possible.

Believing is being

To really inhabit our story, to move the elephant of our hidden hearts, we must embody what we believe. We need to 'do' our story, to put it into action in the form of habits until, eventually, it becomes second nature. Remember that the sexual revolution took root because of the powerful alignment of practising with preaching, especially in LGBT circles. Gay Pride marches may have tested the limits of public tolerance for explicit sexual behaviour, but in every act of defiance there was a powerful moral message too – this is who we are and this is how we will live.

Orthodox Christians must do the same, not as a piece of strategy, but because this is what the gospel demands. Let's start with the vocation to the single life. There's plenty of hand-wringing about singleness in Christian circles, but few churches approach this intentionally and ask what they need to *do*. For some people, a vocation to the single life is a lifelong calling and commitment. Among them will be same-sex attracted followers of Christ who want to live consistently with their religious identity. Others, regardless of their pattern of sexual interests, believe that they best serve the kingdom by remaining single, as did the apostle Paul and Jesus himself, along with some of the greatest Christians of history. There is room for creative thinking about how fellowships can mark, honour and celebrate these commitments more publicly. And there's some important work for the imagination too. Too many of us, including parents, pay lip service to the importance of the single life, while harbouring heart-level idolatries of marriage. We need to reimagine the single life and see as God sees.

Other single people in our church communities are open to the possibility of marriage. In fact, they want to get married as part of their godly calling. This challenges us to think about new opportunities for creative culture making in the sphere of dating. Let me push the envelope a little here. Few minority cultures can survive if they leave the romantic interests of their young people to chance. Look at Orthodox Jews who employ 'match-makers' to facilitate voluntary introductions and help young people navigate their relationships. The individualism of today's evangelicalism, infected by contemporary culture, baulks at such ideas. But those who are faithfully living out a holy vocation of singleness in our sexualized culture need new forms of support and opportunity. Online dating has been a lifeline for many, but it's time for some bolder experiments too.

Finally, what about weddings? These are not meant to be staged evangelistic events, but rather a serious piece of culture making that celebrates what we believe. Too many Christian weddings ape tired middle-class culture: they toast the bridesmaids for 'how beautiful they look', and the men crack jokes while the bride sits passively. There is little here that bears cultural witness to the glory of what is happening before our eyes: a man, forsaking all others to love his wife, bringing his gifts and skills to building a home and caring for children; a woman, equally, bearing the image of God, committing to a lifelong union that will serve and bless the whole community as well. Weddings provide a fertile sphere for creative culture making – in beauty, music and language – that should surprise and inspire every person fortunate enough to have been invited.

How about viewing marriage preparation as one of the first and most important pastoral skills acquired during ministerial training? In today's world every church must provide marriage and parenting courses to enable what is preached from the pulpit to be worked out with the detail it needs. Careful thought will be required for how children are helped to recognize and respect the diversity of views they may encounter at school, while remaining secure and confident in their own Christian identity. And if a fellowship is too small to have its own marriage and parenting seminars and courses, churches must band together to provide them.

If you are a pastor, what are you doing to bring about these life-giving changes in your fellowship? It doesn't need a hammer so much as a whole toolbox of small changes. But you can begin to make some of those changes now. Be ready to listen to others in your congregation who may be better equipped than you. It's a tough call. But unless we are prepared to surrender our people to the cultural power of the revolution, this is something we must address today.

17 BETTER STORYTELLING

We need great storytellers as well as great stories

Do you have childhood memories of being told stories? Curling up in the warm glow of a familiar voice that transports you to another world? Some people were better at it than others, weren't they? They were the naturals. The story had to be a good one, of course, but some storytellers could turn it into a great one. And so, in our response to the sexual revolution, we need better storytelling as well as a better story.

Over the past two to three decades our tone has often sounded harsh and uncaring. Self-absorbed, even. For example, when we talked about freedom of speech, we sometimes created the impression that the only freedom we cared about was our own. We need better storytelling than this. So, as we reach the end of this book, we are going to explore the four hallmarks of good storytelling.

Good storytelling

Listen to those who differ from you
First, we need to be good listeners as well as talkers. In the culture wars there has often been too much 'answering' and

too little 'listening', on all sides. There is a fundamental biblical principle here: 'To answer before listening – that is folly and shame' (Proverbs 18:13). Of course, circling the wagons feels good. And bunkering down with people who think like you makes you feel safe. But although demonizing your opponent from a safe distance can satisfy the emotions, it doesn't focus the mind. Our ideas and ideals won't be strengthened unless they are properly tested. And so we need to heed Scripture's call to listen before we speak, and stand ready to respect the good faith of those who may hold views different from our own.

Of course, we mustn't be taken for fools either. Activists on all sides of the debate will use all their powers in the dark art of persuasion. And, as we saw in the last chapter, listening can't be allowed to stave off decision for ever. Where important matters are at stake, sooner or later you have to make up your mind and walk through the lobbies. But if we want to be better storytellers, we need to understand where our audience is coming from. That is why I have spent so much time in this book trying to understand how people feel and think about these issues. This brings us to the second hallmark of good storytelling.

Know your audience

Because of the cultural power of today's progressive moral agenda, some people argue that rather than wasting diminishing resources on the hopeless task of convincing the wider world, Christians should concentrate their firepower on preserving their moral convictions and ways of life among themselves. One example is the 'Benedict Option', an idea of US author and journalist Rod Dreher.[1]

Dreher believes that the cultural power aligned against orthodox beliefs is now so strong that it is likely that those who hold to them will soon be excluded from the public square. Given the power of culture to shape hearts and minds, Dreher believes that Christians need to pay much more attention to sustaining their own beliefs in community. When barbarian invaders sacked Rome and destroyed its culture, Benedictine monks preserved the Christian faith by retreating into communities that safeguarded their beliefs and ways of life, and something like that is needed now, argues Dreher. Hence, the 'Benedict Option'.

Other Christians perceive the Benedict Option as being too disposed to 'batten down the hatches'. A suggested alternative – let's call it the 'Wilberforce Option' – holds that Christians must never be silenced from the public square: their faith demands that they bear witness to the cross of Christ and fight injustice wherever it is found. The blood of the martyrs has won the freedoms we enjoy today, they insist, and now it is our time to stand up and be counted. In the sphere of sex and relationships, we must speak up for children and for the poorest, because that is what our faith requires.

Benedict versus Wilberforce
So which is it to be, Benedict or Wilberforce? I think it needs to be both. Realistically, in the short term, most of our energy will need to be expended on preserving confidence in our own communities. As we saw in the last chapter, there is much work to be done in transforming our own communities in ways that will buttress and nurture what we believe. But while sustaining and nurturing these beliefs must be our short-term priority, our hearts, together with our heads, must remain orientated to the welfare of the city where we have been exiled. Clearly, some are better gifted for building convictions inside the Christian community, whereas others are better equipped for engagement in the public square.

Let's make sure that we have the right storytellers working in the right context.

Employ artists as well as apologists

The third hallmark of good storytelling involves the use of media that will engage with our culture and capture the imagination. We live in a strongly visual culture, used to relatively short messages with a strong narrative format. So good storytelling needs artists as well as gifted apologists.

As we've seen, the introduction of gay marriage in the UK arguably owes more to programmes like *Will and Grace* than careful rational argument. So, as our confidence in the Christian vision grows, we shall see a new generation of Christian artists producing a range of visually engaging materials too. There are some encouraging examples already available.[2]

We shouldn't, however, restrict artistry to those who work in visual or theatrical media. In a sense we are all artists – culture makers – charged with living out our convictions in the grace-filled dramas of our own life and community. This does not replace rational argument and the need to make our case winsomely. We need both – agents of truth and artists who portray its beauty and grace.

Speaking with grace and truth

Fourth, and finally, good storytelling in the area of sex and relationships needs to embody both truth and grace. Truth is what God sees – the unyielding facts of who he is, who we are, and the realities we inhabit. Grace is how he sees – by offering free and uncompromising forgiveness, love and compassion. In the gospel you can't have one without the other. You can't have a bit of one and a bit of the other either. It's 100 per cent of both: 'We have seen his glory, the glory of the one and only Son, who came from the Father, full of grace and truth' (John 1:14).

I have heard it suggested that in the sphere of sex and relationships we are called to be 'orthodox in our doctrine but liberal in our love'. This is simply a terrible mistake. It divides truth from grace. Worse, it cedes love and compassion to the liberal cause while retaining doctrine for the conservative side. But doctrine that does not speak of love is not truly orthodox at all. And so we must insist on being orthodox in doctrine and therefore orthodox in love, compassion and grace.

But what does this look like? In the sphere of sex and relationships this means a 100-per-cent commitment to truth in what God has revealed about reality. Our convictions need to be set out clearly and then meshed into the everyday discourse of our fellowship at an *assumed* level. We must reflect on how we can nurture and strengthen truth-telling in our Christian communities, because unless we inhabit our beliefs in this way, the power of culture will soon make them captive once again.

Let's try to embody our convictions in the daily rhythms and liturgies of our lives as well. We must teach them to our children, discuss them in our homes and small groups, and proclaim them from our pulpits, with compassion and sensitivity. Each level requires a different set of storytelling skills, but together they consolidate the whole picture: this is where we stand.

At the same time as holding to truth, we need to be 100 per cent grace. So we try to offer the forbearance and acceptance that God has shown us, as surely as we embody the truth that makes it possible. Nobody is excluded from the arms of God's grace. Grace is the ultimate level playing field, the final inclusion. Of course, grace accepts us as we are, but it doesn't leave us as we are. It calls us into submission to the truth, all of it, about God and about ourselves. In the sphere of sex and relationships we are all stumblers; the difference between us is a matter of degree, that's all. And so our churches must practise 'big-tent hospitality' that includes all who hear the call of Jesus and stumble to bear his image in their lives.

What might this look like?

The big tent of God's grace

Given the huge cultural change brought about by the revolution, we have some hard thinking ahead if our churches are going to practise big-tent hospitality. Each church needs to think through its principles and convictions with regard to divorce and remarriage, cohabitation and, increasingly, gender identity issues. This step alone will pose tough questions, and even among churches with a clear orthodox stance, there are likely to be differences of emphasis and application, for example, in terms of qualifications for Communion and leadership. We are going to need to accept a degree of messiness here. In fact, in this area the idea of 'messy church' is taken to a whole new level!

Let's look briefly at just a few issues that could arise. Take the case of a divorced man who left his wife for his secretary and later remarried. He now expresses genuine repentance about the affair. He and his new wife offer to help with marriage preparation. What would you say? Or think of a church plant (known to me) that has built up to seventy regular attenders on a tough housing estate: already, two newcomers are in a same-sex partnership and another has declared himself transgender. How would you hold together your convictions while ensuring that your fellowship offers welcome and support? Or take the example of a pastor I met whose son had come out as gay, entered into a civil marriage and adopted a child with his partner. 'He is my grandson,' the pastor told me, 'and I love that kid with all my heart.' How would you navigate that reality? Or think about a same-sex couple who turn up at your church having adopted a disabled child. One of them becomes a committed Christian. They are warm, kind and generous people. They want to have the child baptized. Now what?[3]

I think we need to begin viewing these situations as God-given opportunities rather than problems. Of course, we shouldn't underestimate the scale of the challenge that lies ahead: human psychology makes it hard to hold two conflicting emotions in your mind at the same time. Take a situation where you love your daughter more than you can say, but she is in a form of relationship that you can't endorse. How do you love freely without compromising your convictions?

I think the answer is to look at Jesus, who modelled this kind of grace on a daily basis. First, reaffirm your commitment to God's ways; centre it in your heart with conviction. Then imagine your daughter as made in the image of God, no matter how broken and disfigured, and love her with all your heart. Remember your own brokenness. Remember how much God loves and cares for her. Pray for her. You don't need to rehearse your convictions over again; she knows what you think. Instead, go the extra mile to serve her and respect her choices. Through the pain of emotional dissonance, stay centred in God's grace and truth, and, gradually, with time and effort, it gets easier. Just do it. For the sake of Christ.

As we navigate these issues, we can learn from the past too. Take polygamy. Some missions did great damage by failing to recognize the support systems woven into the practice of polygamy, especially for women and children. If a husband and his wives come to faith, you cannot simply unravel a polygamous family arrangement overnight that involves so many interdependencies, especially concerning children. Other missions behaved more sensibly, implementing various degrees of pastoral accommodation while holding firm to their convictions about the nature of marriage. So, for example, converts in polygamous relationships could be welcomed into church membership and baptism, provided they publicly subscribed to the church's traditional teaching on marriage and vowed to enter into no more polygamous liaisons. And while polygamists could become full members, they could not take on significant leadership responsibilities.

These are just some examples of the challenges and opportunities we face as we learn how to hold together grace and truth.

Messy church

Welcome to messy church. Maybe you are beginning to feel this is all looking a bit too messy. But that's how it works. God's grace invades the sometimes ugly, always messy, realities of all lives to make them whole. And, gently but firmly, his grace guides us home in truth. That is the reality we must embrace.

I remember once flying home from Israel and finding myself sitting next to an archaeologist who had been supervising a dig in Galilee. I was telling him how I had found the Church of the Holy Sepulchre – reputedly built on the place of Jesus' crucifixion – an unholy mayhem of tourists, touts and wailing liturgists competing to make their voices heard above the rest. What a mess, I complained.

He smiled. 'But wasn't that just like the day of the crucifixion . . . milling crowds, cat-calling Pharisees, brutal soldiers, wailing women, curious tourists and throngs of disinterested travellers passing by? It was just one unholy mess as well.'

And so it was. But it was a mess out of which God's grace brought life for the world.

At the beginning of this book we asked whether the revival of the Christian moral vision is simply a pipe dream. Maybe you still find it hard to respond with much confidence. But we have been here before. Two thousand years ago, after Jesus' ascension, it seemed that he had left his mission in the hands of an ill-equipped team of incompetents. And yet the belief that Jesus of Nazareth had been raised from the dead inspired this small band of Christians to create a culture so attractive to pagans – by the way they treated women, children, the sexually exploited, slaves and the poor – that by the end of the fourth century an empire was on the verge of belief. We shall need to pray. We shall need to think very hard. Many questions will remain. But for the sake of the gospel, for the life of the world, the biblical moral vision is a story we must now be prepared to tell all over again.

NOTES

What lies ahead

1. http://www.irishcentral.com/news/2000-irish-children-were-illegally-adopted-in-us-from-magdalene-laundries-189789961-237563011.html. Accessed 4 February 2016.
2. http://www.cso.ie/en/newsandevents/pressreleases/2015pressreleases/pressreleasebirthsdeathsandmarriagesin2014/. Accessed 4 February 2016.
3. http://www.belfasttelegraph.co.uk/news/northern-ireland/six-in-ten-northern-ireland-babies-are-now- born-outside-wedlock-31550726.html. Accessed 4 February 2016.
4. http://www.newstatesman.com/politics/2013/07/i-oppose-tax-breaks-marriage—why-should-i-subsidise-other-people's-weird-lifesty. Accessed 4 February 2016.
5. http://www.telegraph.co.uk/news/religion/7668448/Christian-preacher-arrested-for-saying-homosexuality-is-a-sin.html. Accessed 1 May 2010.

1 Revolution is my name

1. For a brief overview, see W. Bradford Wilcox, Nicholas H. Wolfinger and Charles E. Stokes (2015), http://family-studies.org/the-role-of-culture-in-declining-marriage-rates/?utm_content=buffer3d14a&utm_medium=social&utm_source=twitter.com&utm_campaign=buffer. Accessed 17 March 2016.

2. Gray 2006: 662.

3. Gillon 2004: Introduction.

4. Harrison 2013.

5. Tanya Branigan, 'Keys to the Good Life',
   http://www.theguardian.com/uk/2006/jul/04/
   internationalaidanddevelopment.g8. Accessed 6 November
   2015.

2 The ideology of the revolution

1. Marx 1970.

2. Berger 1969.

3. http://www.bbc.co.uk/news/business-35842808. Accessed
   22 March 2016.

4. http://nymag.com/news/features/45938/. Accessed 30 June
   2016.

5. Wright 2013: 9.

6. Ibid. 6.

7. Quoted from Burfeind 2014, http://thefederalist.com/2015/
   06/29/gnostic-mysticism-grounds-modern-progressive-
   ideology/. Accessed 21 December 2015.

8. A compelling analysis of the Gnostic revolution of modern
   culture can be found in Burfeind 2014.

9. http://www.nytimes.com/2015/10/11/magazine/the-year-
   we-obsessed-over-identity.html?_r=0. Accessed 14 December
   2015.

10. http://www.independent.co.uk/news/world/americas/
    stefonknee-wolschtt-transgender-father-leaves-family-in-
    toronto-to-start-new-life-as-a-six-year-old-a6769051.html.
    Accessed 12 December 2015.

11. http://www.telegraph.co.uk/news/worldnews/
    northamerica/usa/11678667/Rachel-Dolezal-who-pretended-
    to-be-African-American-says-she-identifies-as-black.html.
    Accessed 12 December 2015.

12. http://www.telegraph.co.uk/news/newstopics/
    howaboutthat/12127067/woman-says-she-is-a-cat-
    trapped-in-the-wrong-body.html. Accessed 4 February
    2016.
13. Some of the material in this chapter is taken from an earlier
    paper: G. Harrison, 'Who Am I Today?', Cambridge Papers
    (Jubilee Centre, 2016).
14. Lewis 1999.
15. Ibid. 12.

3 The moral vision of the revolution

1. http://www.theguardian.com/world/2015/sep/02/
   shocking-image-of-drowned-syrian-boy-shows-tragic-plight-
   of-refugees. Accessed 5 November 2015.
2. Haidt 2012.
3. Kahneman 2012.
4. Haidt 2012: 38, referring to the work of neuroscientist
   Antonio Damasio.
5. Ibid. 131ff.
6. Technically, these reactions are a particular type of
   preconscious 'emotionally connected' cognition, rather than
   representing pure emotion.
7. This story is based on a similar fictional story used by
   Haidt, but brought up to date in this widely reported, but
   uncorroborated, incident: https://en.wikipedia.org/wiki/
   Piggate. Accessed 5 November 2015.
8. http://www.publications.parliament.uk/pa/cm201415/
   cmhansrd/cm150203/debtext/150203-0002.htm. Accessed
   17 November 2015.

4 The storytellers of the revolution

1. http://www.ncbi.nlm.nih.gov/pubmed/19580564. Accessed
   29 December 2015.

2. http://www.sciencedirect.com/science/article/pii/
S0167268111000163. Accessed 29 December 2015.

3. Campbell 1972. Originally published 1949.

4. http://www.jcf.org/new/index.php?categoryid=83&p9999_
action=details&p9999_wid=692. Accessed 29 December
2015.

5. We should note that this was a real-life situation: this father
really did experience the suffering shown and the boy did
eventually die.

6. Zacks 2014.

7. Smith 2014.

8. Ibid. 24.

9. http://www.thetimes.co.uk/tto/opinion/columnists/
timmontgomerie/article3625882.ece. Accessed 28 December
2015.

5 The narrative of the revolution

1. http://greatergood.berkeley.edu/article/item/how_stories_
change_brain. Accessed 30 December 2015.

2. Gladwell 2013.

3. https://www.youtube.com/watch?v=a54UBWFXsF4.
Accessed 30 December 2015.

4. Although it was later easily overtaken by Sam Smith's 'Lay
Me Down', which had over 127 million views when accessed
30 December 2015.

5. In the US support among 'white evangelical protestants
reached 24% in 2015 and 62% among mainline protestants',
http://www.pewforum.org/2015/07/29/graphics-slideshow-
changing-attitudes-on-gay-marriage/. Accessed 31 December
2015. Reliable data for the UK are not readily available. A 2015
survey commissioned by Oasis Trust generated newspaper
headlines, but appears not to have defined its sample very
clearly: http://www.telegraph.co.uk/news/religion/

11482876/Churchgoers-keeping-liberal-views-on-
homosexuality-secret.html. Accessed 27 June 2016.
6. http://acl.asn.au/resources/dr-ashley-null-on-thomas-
cranmer/. Accessed 27 June 2016.

6 The warriors of the revolution
1. http://www.stonewall.org.uk/people/ian-mckellen.
Accessed 27 November 2015.
2. Issenberg 2012.
3. http://www.nytimes.com/2012/11/13/health/dream-
team-of-behavioral-scientists-advised-obama-campaign.html.
Accessed 9 December 2015.
4. http://news.bbc.co.uk/1/hi/uk/77536.stm. Accessed
25 November 2015.
5. Homan 1999.
6. http://www.christianitytoday.com/ct/2015/march/
andy-crouch-gospel-in-age-of-public-shame.html. Accessed
2 July 2016.
7. Ibid.

7 The casualties of the revolution
1. Berger 1969.
2. Bond and Smith 1996. In this meta-analysis of similar studies
on social conformity the authors confirmed that Asch's
findings were robust. However, rates of social conformity
appear to have declined in the West (compared with other
societies) over the past half-century.
3. https://www.youtube.com/watch?v=NyDDyT1lDhA.
Accessed 25 November 2015.

8 The plank in your own eye
1. http://www.newstatesman.com/node/195223. Accessed
13 January 2016.

2. http://www.ncbi.nlm.nih.gov/pubmed/9499570. Accessed 13 January 2016.

3. Wuthnow 2010: 140.

4. https://web.archive.org/web/20080610111907/ http://www.barna.org/FlexPage.aspx?Page= BarnaUpdate&BarnaUpdateID=295. Accessed 13 January 2016.

5. See a review at http://family-studies.org/findings-on-red-and-blue-divorce-are-not-exactly-black-and-white/. Accessed 14 January 2016.

6. W. Bradford Wilcox and E. Williamson, 'The Cultural Contradictions of Mainline Family Ideology and Practice', in Browning and Clairmont 2007: 50.

7. Shaw 2015: 104.

8. http://www.redeemer.com/redeemer-report/article/ the_bible_and_same_sex_relationships_a_review_article. Accessed 30 March 2016.

9 Sleeping with the enemy

1. For example, Matthew Vines makes this point forcibly and with some justification: 'I have spoken repeatedly against the notion that "be yourself" is a sufficient Christian ethic': http://www.matthewvines.com/a-response-to-tim-kellers-review/. Accessed 27 June 2016.

2. Spiegelhalter 2015.

3. Ibid. 20.

4. http://www.independent.co.uk/life-style/love-sex/ gym-used-as-a-hook-up-spot-as-a-quarter-of-adults-admit-to-having-sex-there-a6806246.html. Accessed 15 January 2016.

5. http://www.independent.co.uk/life-style/gadgets-and-tech/ world-cup-passions-in-brazil-give-a-boost-to-dating-apps-tinder-and-grindr-9562309.html. Accessed 15 January 2016.

6. http://www.theguardian.com/lifeandstyle/2014/sep/28/
   -sp-not-tonight-darling-why-britain-having-less-sex. Accessed
   15 January 2016.
7. Putnam 2000.
8. http://www.ons.gov.uk/peoplepopulationandcommunity/
   birthsdeathsandmarriages/families/bulletins/
   familiesandhouseholds/2015-11-05#living. Accessed 10 April
   2016.
9. Quoted in http://www.telegraph.co.uk/women/
   womens-life/9930325/Being-single-by-choice-is-liberating-
   says-Hannah-Betts.html. Accessed 2 July 2016.
10. Lewis 1977: 19–20.

10 War on the weak

1. Putnam 2015.
2. http://www.christianpost.com/news/harvard-professor-
   robert-putnam-on-rich-poor-opportunity-gap-kids-need-
   two-parents-churches-can-do-more-than-government-cp-
   interview-2-2-137089/. Accessed 9 February 2016.
3. http://www.spectator.co.uk/2014/11/marriage-is-becoming-
   a-preserve-of-the-rich/. Accessed 9 February 2016.
4. http://www.theatlantic.com/magazine/archive/1926/07/
   the-russian-effort-to-abolish-marriage/306295/. Accessed
   9 February 2016. I am grateful to Joe Carter for his blog
   on this issue, which can be found here: http://www.
   thegospelcoalition.org/article/the-communist-roots-of-no-
   fault-divorce. Accessed 9 February 2016.
5. http://stateofourunions.org/2010/when-marriage-
   disappears.php. Accessed 10 February 2016.
6. Ibid.
7. http://www.futureofchildren.org/futureofchildren/
   publications/docs/Marriage%20Revisited%20Introduction.pdf.
   Accessed 10 February 2016.

8. Ibid.

9. http://www.princeton.edu/futureofchildren/publications/docs/WhyMarriageMatters.pdf. Accessed 10 February 2016.

10. For a good summary of the data, see Spiegelhalter 2015: 43–47.

11. http://www.familylaw.co.uk/system/redactor_assets/documents/2619/ONS_families_and_households2014_statstical_bulletin.pdf. Accessed 10 February 2016.

12. In fact, high-conflict warring couples are a relative rarity among those who decide to split: the vast majority involve low-conflict situations. http://www.marriagefoundation.org.uk/Shared/Uploads/Products/37543_MF%20paper%20-%20Out%20of%20the%20blue%20divorces.pdf. Accessed 10 February 2016.

13. http://www.marriagefoundation.org.uk/Web/Content/Default.aspx?Content=441. Accessed 10 February 2016.

14. http://www.centreforsocialjustice.org.uk/UserStorage/pdf/Pdf%20reports/FamilyBreakdownIsNotAboutDivorce.pdf. Accessed 10 February 2016.

15. http://www.pewsocialtrends.org/2011/06/15/a-tale-of-two-fathers/. Accessed 10 February 2016.

16. http://www.childrenscommissioner.gov.uk/sites/default/files/publications/Basically_porn_is_everywhere.pdf. Accessed 30 March 2016.

17. Ibid. 22.

11 Who am I today?

1. G. Harrison, 'Who Am I Today?', Cambridge Papers (Jubilee Centre, 2016), http://www.jubilee-centre.org/10178-2/. Accessed 20 May 2016. (This chapter is largely based upon this paper.)

2. P. Biggs, 'Emerging Issues for Our Hyperconnected World', in S. Dutta and B. Bilbao-Osorio (eds.), *The Global Information*

Technology Report 2012: Living in a Hyperconnected World,
World Economic Forum Insight Report [online]. Available
from: http://www3.weforum.org/docs/Global_IT_
Report_2012.pdf. Accessed 1 February 2016.

3. http://www.aafprs.org/media/stats_polls/m_stats.html.
Accessed 5 February 2016.

4. See R. Cooper (2009), *Alter Ego: Avatars and Their Creators*
(London: Chris Boot Ltd).

5. http://www.bbc.com/news/health-30414589. Accessed
20 January 2016.

6. http://pss.sagepub.com/content/20/7/860.abstract.
Accessed 20 January 2016.

7. Harrison 2013.

8. Yarhouse 2015. A brief introduction to gender dysphoria
considered from a Christian standpoint can also be
downloaded from here: https://www.cmf.org.uk/resources/
publications/content/?context=article&id=26419. Accessed
16 May 2016.

12 Living in God's reality

1. It's notable that after the fall God 'cursed . . . the ground',
leading to 'thorns and thistles' and work carried out 'by the
sweat of your brow'. The harmony between humans and
the world in which they had been placed has been broken
(Genesis 3:17–19).

2. Book 1, epistle x, line 24.

13 The end of longing

1. http://www.theguardian.com/books/2002/jan/12/books.
guardianreview5. Accessed 27 June 2016.

2. https://wikiislam.net/wiki/72_Virgins. Accessed 4 July
2015.

3. Lewis 1974: 163.

4. For an overview of the evidence, see
   https://www.researchgate.net/profile/Andrew_Lewis3/
   publication/222112117_The_role_of_oxytocin_in_mother_
   infant_relations_a_systematic_review_of_human_studies/
   links/odeec53146b43aaf37000000.pdf. Accessed 23 February
   2016.
5. https://en.wikipedia.org/wiki/Trinity_(Andrei_Rublev).
   Accessed 2 April 2016.
6. Smith 2009: 75.
7. Augustine of Hippo (354–430), *Confessions*, Book 1.
8. Smith 2009: 76–77.

14 The end of shame

1. Lewis 1965: 98.
2. Williams and Hadfield 1990: 70.
3. Alighieri 2012, tr. Robin Kirkpatrick.
4. Smith 2009: 79, note 7.
5. Grant 2015: 230.

15 For the life of the world

1. Kuehne 2009: 117.
2. Bakke 2005.
3. Ibid. 44.
4. For a wonderful set of resources supporting a vision of
   'Life for the World', see http://www.letterstotheexiles.com.
   Accessed 15 April 2016.
5. Letter from Birmingham Jail, 16 April 1963.

16 Our better story

1. For example, see Gagnon 2001.
2. Lewis 1965: 109.

17 Better storytelling

1. For a good summary, see http://www.theamericanconservative.com/dreher/benedict-option-faq/. Accessed 5 April 2016.

2. For example, see the 'For the Life of the World' resource referred to earlier, http://www.letterstotheexiles.com.

3. One of the best pastoral resources for dealing with these complex situations is Goddard and Horrocks 2012.

SOME RESOURCES AND FURTHER READING

On sex and marriage

Ash, Christopher, *Marriage: Sex in the Service of God* (Inter-Varsity Press, 2003)

Grant, Jonathan, *Divine Sex: A Compelling Vision for Christian Relationships in a Hypersexualized Age* (Brazos Press, 2015)

Keller, Timothy, with Kathy Keller, *The Meaning of Marriage: Facing the Complexities of Commitment with the Wisdom of God* (Hodder & Stoughton, 2011)

Winner, Lauren, *Real Sex: The Naked Truth about Chastity* (Brazos Press, 2005)

On bisexuality and same-sex attraction

Gagnon, Robert A. J., *The Bible and Homosexual Practice: Texts and Hermeneutics* (Abingdon Press, 2002)

Goddard, Andrew, and Don Horrocks (eds.), *Resources for Church Leaders: Biblical and Pastoral Responses to Homosexuality* (Evangelical Alliance, 2012)

Hill, Wesley, *Washed and Waiting: Reflections on Christian Faithfulness and Homosexuality* (Zondervan, 2010)

Living Out website has a range of useful resources: http://www.livingout.org/stories

Selmys, Melinda, *Sexual Authenticity: An Intimate Reflection on Homosexuality and Catholicism* (Our Sunday Visitor, 2009)

Shaw, Ed, *The Plausibility Problem: The Church and Same-Sex Attraction* (Inter-Varsity Press, 2015)

On identity and transgender

Harrison, Glynn, 'Who Am I Today? The Modern Crisis of Identity', Cambridge Papers (Jubilee Centre, 2016), http://www.jubilee-centre.org/10178-2/

Thomas, Rick, and Peter Saunders, 'Gender Dysphoria', CMF Files, no. 59 (Christian Medical Fellowship, 2016), http://admin.cmf.org.uk/pdf/cmffiles/59_gender_dysphoria.pdf

Yarhouse, Mark A., *Understanding Gender Dysphoria: Navigating Transgender Issues in a Changing Culture* (IVP Academic, 2015)

BIBLIOGRAPHY

Alighieri, D. (2012), *The Divine Comedy: Inferno, Purgatorio, Paradiso*, tr. R. Kirkpatrick, London: Penguin Classics.

Ariely, D. (2008), *Predictably Irrational: The Hidden Forces that Shape Our Decisions*, New York: HarperCollins.

Bakke, O. M. (2005), *When Children Became People: The Birth of Childhood in Early Christianity*, Minneapolis: Fortress Press.

Becker, C. L. (1966), *The Heavenly City of the Eighteenth-Century Philosophers*, New Haven: Yale University Press.

Berger, P. L. (1969), *A Rumor of Angels: Modern Society and the Rediscovery of the Supernatural*, New York: Doubleday.

Bersoff, D. M. (1999), 'Why Good People Sometimes Do Bad Things: Motivated Reasoning and Unethical Behavior', *Personality and Social Psychology Bulletin* 25.1: 28–39. doi: 10.1177/0146167299025001003.

Bond, R. and P. B. Smith (1996), 'Culture and Conformity: A Meta-Analysis of Studies Using Asch's (1952b, 1956) Line Judgment Task', *Psychological Bulletin* 119.1: 111–137. doi: 10.1037/0033-2909.119.1.111.

Branigan, T, 'Keys to the Good Life', http://www.theguardian.com/uk/2006/jul/04/internationalaidanddevelopment.g8. Accessed 6 November 2015.

Browning, D. S. and D. A. Clairmont (eds.) (2007), *American Religions and the Family: How Faith Traditions Cope with Modernization and Democracy*, New York: Columbia University Press.

Burfeind, P. M. (2014), *Gnostic America: A Reading of Contemporary American Culture & Religion According to Christianity's Oldest Heresy*, Toledo: Pax Domini Press.

Campbell, J. (1972), *The Hero with a Thousand Faces*, Princeton, NJ: Princeton University Press.

Dostoyevsky, F. (1963), *Crime and Punishment*, New York: Dodd, Mead.

Drury, J. and S. D. Reicher (2010), 'Crowd Control', *Scientific American Mind* 21.5: 58–65. doi:10.1038/ scientificamericanmind1110-58.

Gagnon, R. A. J. (2001), *The Bible and Homosexual Practice: Texts and Hermeneutics*, Nashville: Abingdon Press.

Gillon, S. M. (2004), *Boomer Nation: The Largest and Richest Generation Ever and How It Changed America*, New York: Free Press.

Gladwell, M. (2013), *David and Goliath: Underdogs, Misfits, and the Art of Battling Giants*, London: Penguin.

Goddard, A. and D. Horrocks (2012), *Resources for Church Leaders: Biblical and Pastoral Responses to Homosexuality*, London: Evangelical Alliance.

Grant, J. (2015), *Divine Sex: A Compelling Vision for Christian Relationships in a Hypersexualized Age*, Grand Rapids: Brazos Press.

Gray, M. (2006), *The Bob Dylan Encyclopedia*, New York: Continuum.

Haidt, J. (2012), *The Righteous Mind: Why Good People Are Divided by Politics and Religion*, New York: Pantheon Books.

Harrison, G. (2013), *The Big Ego Trip: Finding True Significance in a Culture of Self-Esteem*, Nottingham: Inter-Varsity Press.

Hart, D. B. (2013), *The Experience of God: Being, Consciousness, Bliss*, New York and London: Yale University Press.

Homan, M. S. (1999), *Promoting Community Change: Making It Happen in the Real World*, Pacific Grove, CA: Brooks/Cole.

Hume, D. (1777), 'An Enquiry Concerning Human Understanding', *David Hume: Enquiries Concerning Human Understanding and Concerning the Principles of Morals (Third Edition)*, 5. doi:10.1093/oseo/instance.00046350.

———— (1966), *An Enquiry Concerning the Principles of Morals*, La Salle, IL: Open Court.

Issenberg, S. (2012), *The Victory Lab: The Secret Science of Winning Campaigns*, New York: Crown.

Kahneman, D. (2012), *Thinking, Fast and Slow*, London: Penguin.

Klinenberg, E. (2012), *Going Solo: The Extraordinary Rise and Surprising Appeal of Living Alone*, New York: Penguin.

Kuehne, D. S. (2009), *Sex and the iWorld: Rethinking Relationship beyond an Age of Individualism*, Grand Rapids: Baker Academic.

Leary, M. R. (2004), *The Curse of the Self: Self-Awareness, Egotism, and the Quality of Human Life*, Oxford: Oxford University Press.

Lewis, C. S. (1965), *Screwtape Proposes a Toast, and Other Pieces*, London: Collins.

———— (1970), *God in the Dock: Essays on Theology and Ethics*, Grand Rapids: Eerdmans.

———— (1974), *Miracles*, Glasgow: William Collins.

———— (1977), *The Great Divorce*, London: Fount.

———— (1999), *The Abolition of Man*, London: Fount.

MacCulloch, D. (2003), *Reformation: Europe's House Divided, 1490–1700*, London: Allen Lane.

Marx, K. (1970), *A Contribution to the Critique of Political Economy*, New York: International Publishers.

Mill, J. S. and E. Rapaport (1978), *On Liberty*, Indianapolis: Hackett Publishing.

Packer, J. I. and N. T. Wright (2008), *Anglican Evangelical Identity: Yesterday and Today*, London: Latimer Trust.

Parada, H. and M. S. Homan (2011), *Promoting Community Change: Making It Happen in the Real World*, Toronto: Nelson Education.

Powers, K. (2015), *The Silencing: How the Left Is Killing Free Speech*, Washington, DC: Regnery Publishing.

Putnam, R. D. (2000), *Bowling Alone: The Collapse and Revival of American Community*, New York: Simon & Schuster.

―――― (2015), *Our Kids: The American Dream in Crisis*, New York: Simon & Schuster.

Regnerus, M. D. (2007), *Forbidden Fruit: Sex & Religion in the Lives of American Teenagers*, Oxford: Oxford University Press.

Ricoeur, P. (1992), *Oneself as Another*, Chicago: University of Chicago Press.

Shaw, E. (2015), *The Plausibility Problem: The Church and Same-Sex Attraction*, Nottingham: Inter-Varsity Press.

Slovic, P., M. L. Finucane, E. Peters and D. G. MacGregor (2006), 'The Affect Heuristic', *The Construction of Preference*, 434–453. doi:10.1017/cbo9780511618031.024.

Smith, J. K. A. (2009), *Desiring the Kingdom: Worship, Worldview, and Cultural Formation*, Grand Rapids: Baker Academic.

―――― (2014), *How (Not) to Be Secular: Reading Charles Taylor*, Grand Rapids: Eerdmans.

Spiegelhalter, D. J. (2015), *Sex by Numbers: What Statistics Can Tell Us about Sexual Behaviour*, London: Profile Books.

Stein, E. (1999), *The Mismeasure of Desire: The Science, Theory, and Ethics of Sexual Orientation*, Oxford: Oxford University Press.

Todorov, A. (2005), 'Candidates' "Face Value" Could Influence Voter Behavior', Woodrow Wilson School of Public and International Affairs, http://wws.princeton.edu/node/8993. Accessed 7 November 2015.

Via, D. O. and R. A. J. Gagnon (2003), *Homosexuality and the Bible: Two Views*, Minneapolis: Fortress Press.

Williams, C. and A. M. Hadfield (1990), *Outlines of Romantic Theology*, Grand Rapids: Eerdmans.

Wright, T. (2013), *Creation, Power and Truth: The Gospel in a World of Cultural Confusion*, London: SPCK.

Wuthnow, R. (2010), *After the Baby Boomers: How Twenty- and Thirty-Somethings Are Shaping the Future of American Religion*, Princeton, NJ: Princeton University Press.

Yarhouse, M. A. (2015), *Understanding Gender Dysphoria: Navigating Transgender Issues in a Changing Culture*, Downers Grove: Inter-Varsity Press.

YouGov (2015), '1 in 2 Young People Say They Are Not 100% Heterosexual', https://yougov.co.uk/news/2015/08/16/half-young-not-heterosexual/. Accessed 5 November 2015.

Zacks, J. M. (2014), *Flicker: Your Brain on Movies*, New York: Oxford University Press.